IMAGES
of America

GILFORD

MAP OF GILFORD. This 1892 map of Gilford is from *Atlas of the State of New Hampshire*, compiled by D.H. Hurd & Co., Boston. It was enclosed in Adair Mulligan's Gunstock Parish book, 1995. It includes the Lake Shore Railroad, Lakeport, and parts of Paugus Bay. (Courtesy of the Gilford Public Library, New Hampshire Room.)

ON THE COVER: THE WEEKS FARM. This photograph is from the Weeks family farm on Weeks Road, courtesy of Peter Weeks. The photograph came from an old chest kept in the upper corner bedroom, which was once Peter's room when he was a child. The pictures there belonged to his mother, Mildred "Millie" Weeks. Peter describes this scene as "the old shed in the back field, next to part of the corn crib. Late 1800s. Most likely the workers from the blueberry fields that once were a big part of the harvest time in Gilford." Peter is the fifth generation of Weeks family to run the old 1837 dairy farm. At its height, the farm produced 1,400 pounds of milk and had a herd of 26 cows, Peter reports. He fondly remembers the days gone by of pigs, sheep, chickens, hay, and a team of horses called Squirrel and Jenny. Peter's parents, Arthur and Millie, remained active in the town throughout their lives. (Courtesy of Peter Weeks, Weeks Farm Collection.)

IMAGES
of America

GILFORD

Doris L. Chitty and Geoffrey B. Ruggles
Foreword by Sheldon C. Morgan

ARCADIA
PUBLISHING

Published by Arcadia Publishing
Charleston, South Carolina

Library of Congress Control Number: 2015935771

For all general information, please contact Arcadia Publishing:
Telephone 843-853-2070
Fax 843-853-0044
E-mail sales@arcadiapublishing.com
For customer service and orders:
Toll-Free 1-888-313-2665

Visit us on the Internet at www.arcadiapublishing.com

This book is dedicated to the Gilford historians, all those that, in some
way, have helped to preserve Gilford's past, and Sheldon C. Morgan, past
director of public works, health officer, and cemetery steward. During
his 43 years of service, he promoted and protected the past by creating
signage, honoring traditions, and helping with a vast number of projects
such as the Tannery Covered Bridge and Weeks Cemetery restoration.
He protected our parks and memorials. He helped beautify our town by
supporting public gardens and tree planting. We thank you, Sheldon!

CONTENTS

FOREWORD

You are about to delve into a historical journey of photographs that will impart a sense of old New England living and the way things were for our families. You will be brought through a time of change in the newly incorporated small town of Gilford, New Hampshire, and see how transportation, farm living, and the social fabric have evolved over time.

Allow me to introduce myself, my name is Sheldon Morgan, and having been brought up in New Hampshire's lakes region for over 65 years, I was able to see firsthand the way people lived, traveled, and shared values. My family lived adjacent to the railroad and across the road from one of the many lakes in the region. I could see, hear, and smell the way people lived, from the farmlands and its crops to the belch of smoke from an incoming train and the sounds of metal being worked in small factories to tractors and people working the fields and all the other aspects of small-town America. I have dedicated 43 years of my life working in public works, which has allowed me to see the many problems of rural travel people had to endure, the impact weather had on their daily lives, and the social fabric that families maintained to sustain themselves through all trials and tribulations of living the rural life.

As we all go through life attempting to remember our early years and what we believed to be the best of life, this book allows us to see and remember how, not only what our parents went through, but also our grandparents and great-grandparents. If you are like me, you remember the carefree days of growing up and the smells, noises, and even the tastes of your childhood. This book will allow you to see the way families toiled to make a living, the way they lived together, and most of all, the way they grew and accepted life as the best it could be.

Enjoy your tour of memories and the way life used to be.

—Sheldon C. Morgan
Gilford Public Works (retired)

ACKNOWLEDGMENTS

Many people came together to help create a collection of photographs and talk of times past here in Gilford. We need to thank each and every one of you for the time spent sharing stories and memories. Gilford truly has a strong proud group of people who continue to share their family history and knowledge. Although some people remembered here are no longer with us, their photographs will always remain with friends, relatives, and libraries. All of this gives us a glimpse into how our town came to be, the changes throughout time, and a deep appreciation for all the beauty we have here in our town. We cannot thank you enough: Peter Ames, Ames Family Farm, Sandy Bailey, Harry Bean, the Bean family, Ernie Bolduc, the Bolduc family, Bill and Sally Bickford, Shirley Burns, Mary Carter, Judy Cott, the Dinan family, the Goodhue family, Gilford Fire Rescue, Gilford Public Library and its wonderful New Hampshire Room, the Gunstock Inn and Resort, Megan Buckner, Gunstock Recreational Area, Pete and Dorothy LaBonte, the LaBonte family, Diane Mitton, Judy Morgan, Jane Percy, Esther Peters, the Sawyer family, Norm Soucy, the Gilford Village Store, the Thompson-Ames Historical Society, the Laconia Historical Society, Arthur and Peter Weeks, Dr. Kelley Jean White, the Wixson family, Edie Grant, the Grant family, Carole Hunt Johnson, Skip Sanborn, Russell Folsom, Bob Murphy, Frank "Pa" Bates, Charles Davis, the Cummings family, Mrs. Curtis Wilkinson, and a Mrs. York.

We are extremely grateful for the time and photographs from Susan Spearin Leach, cemetery trustee and genealogist, and Merrill Fay of Fay's Boatyard for his priceless collection of photographs, knowledge, and time.

Last, but never least, Sheldon C. Morgan, thank you for always making the time and all your encouragement, proofreading, and support. Without all of you, this project would not have been.

INTRODUCTION

Gilford was once a part of what was called Upper Parish and later Gunstock Parish. Upper Parish in the 1700s included Lakeport, Laconia, Belmont, and what is now known as Gilford. Later, Upper Parish became the Belmont Area. The Gunstock Parish then became Laconia, Lakeport, and today's Gilford. That is why it is known as both parishes in the town history. The Gunstock Recreational Area, Gunstock Inn, and Gunstock Acres have honored and kept the name alive.

On April 10, 1810, a petition was submitted, written by town clerk William Blasdell. The people of Gunstock Parish were tired of traveling and paying for the long trip to town meetings. They want to be their own town. It was voted down on that day. Again, on May 28, 1810, the petition went to town meeting but did not pass. A year went by, and on May 27, 1811, the committee of Nathan Taylor, James McDuffie, and Enoch Wood were sent to create the boundary lines of Gunstock. On March 12, 1812, the vote to set off Gunstock Parish failed. The article to see whether the town would oppose in the legislature the application for creating Gilford was also voted down. The application was successful, and on June 16, 1812, the people could now form a separate town. Lt. Lemuel Mason was the representative to the state legislature. He chose the name Gilford after the 1781 Revolutionary War battle of Guilford Courthouse in North Carolina. Gilford is the only town in New Hampshire named after a Revolutionary War battlefield.

There are three theories as to why the U was omitted from the new name. Some believed the town clerk was so tired after all the paperwork he simply missed the spelling mistake. Some say neither Blasdell nor Mason realized the word had a U in it, and others blamed the statehouse clerk who prepared the final document for making the error. The spelling stayed, and soon the first town officers were elected. Benjamin Weeks and Simeon Hoyt set up a special town meeting. Dudley Ladd was the first moderator. William Blaisdell was elected town clerk. Jacob Randlett, Jacob Blaisdell, and Thomas Saltmarsh were Gilford's first selectmen, and Elder Richard Martin became the representative to the general court. Gilford now had a government.

Gilford was formed as a farming town, different from the surrounding towns. The first meetinghouse was originally built on School House Hill in 1794. Horse, ox, and mule teams were used to clear the massive fields. As the backbreaking chore of creating fields progressed, miles and miles of stone walls were created along the property lines, many of which still remain today. Stunning lake and mountain views could be seen as the farmers worked the land. Ice and lumber were harvested. Cider making and apple picking were popular.

The first few years were tough for many families. In 1813, the spotted fever epidemic hit. For many it was fatal. On November 28 of that year, an earthquake hit. Spotted fever returned in December 1814. A hurricane hit in 1815. Gilford's year without a summer was 1816. Families who lost loved ones within days of each other often buried their family on the same day. Some were buried in the same grave.

Gilford is also unique in the massive number of buildings and homes that were picked up and moved—some across the road, some across town, and some clear across the ice on Lake Winnipesaukee. Quite a task in those days, without the machinery we have today.

The Lake Shore Railroad held opening day on June 17, 1890, Bunker Hill Day. Many of the stops and stations were located in Gilford. Ice was harvested and shipped via rail as well as lumber and farm products. The trains also brought many visitors to town, which opened up an additional way for folks to make ends meet. Many added complete floors to their homes to board and feed those coming to enjoy the beautiful mountains and Lake Winnipesaukee. Boating became busier, and soon steamers and private boats offered their services.

Today, although there are shopping malls and many more homes, there are strong whispers from the past. The heart of Gilford remains protected by the Thompson-Ames Historical Society, the Gilford Village Historic Commission, the Gilford Conservation Commission, and those that care about Gilford's rich past and beautiful land. We are fortunate to have some of the great old homes and buildings standing; some still contain the gunstock corners and hand-hewn beams from the sawmill days. The old bricks and granite posts were all made right here. The Rowe House pines, our cemeteries, and cart roads all bring a piece of history to mind. We protect the small-town close-knit feeling as you travel through the village, back roads, mountain trails, and lakeshores of our town. Many people from all over the United States continue to travel annually to Gilford Old Home Day. Traditions continue to be honored generation after generation.

BICENTENNIAL. Geoff Ruggles (left) and Dee Chitty (right) lead 2012 bicentennial Gilford Old Home Day parade. (Courtesy of Susan Leach.)

One

BEAUTIFUL BELKNAP MOUNTAIN, BRIDGES, AND ROADS

FIRE LOOKOUT TOWER ON MOUNT BELKNAP. The state forest on Mount Belknap consists of approximately 545 acres. The tower was raised 10 feet in 1979, and a new cab was built. Once known as Audrey 8, the tower was a spotting station during World War II. Hikers still set out to reach the tower for magnificent views of Mount Washington, the Winnipesaukee Islands, Portsmouth Harbor, and Mount Wachusett in Vermont. (Courtesy of the Gilford Public Library.)

Lookout Station
Mt.Belknap, Gilford, N.H.

THE VIEW FROM YOUNG ROAD. This view is known to some as Inspiration Point. (Courtesy of Shirley Burns.)

HIKERS ON BELKNAP MOUNTAIN. The Bacon and Weeks families once shared ownership of a pasture on Belknap Mountain Road. Together here resting after their long hike are, from left to right, (first row) F. Milo Bacon, William Weeks, Frank Bacon, and Grace H. Weeks; (second row) Stark Weeks. Grace has a few handmade hiking sticks to her side. It was a relaxing treat to be able to take time out from working to see the view on top of Mount Belknap after a hard work week. (Courtesy of Susan Leach.)

GILFORD BROOK. Gilford Brook runs from the base of Mount Belknap to Lake Winnipesaukee. It enters the lake to the left of Lockes and Rock Island. During the mill era, quite a lot of sawdust was sent down the brook. The owners of the village sawmill, the Morrill family, made money by buying land to cut into lumber and then selling the cut land as pasture. The mill closed in the 1890s. (Courtesy of Gilford Public Library.)

Gilford Brook
240 Gilford, N.H.

WORTH THE HIKE. Imagine for a moment, the task of having to hike up the mountains in a long skirt and sun hat. One's shoes most likely had small heels, and the bottoms were made of slippery leather. These women did not seem to mind. Perhaps the thought of finally reaching the top for such a magnificent view brought added determination. The state began protecting the Belknap Mountain Range in 1928 and by 2009 had 1,629 acres as part of the Belknap Mountain State Forest. (Courtesy of the Laconia Public Library.)

THE BELKNAP MOUNTAIN FIRE WATCHMAN'S CABIN. The Gilford Fire Department was a division of the Public Works Highway Division until 1948. The watchman's cabin was built in 1915 and enlarged in 1934. Nearby there was a 13-foot-deep well with a hand pump. In 1976, Richard "Richie" Stuart started working as watchman in the cabin and lived there in 1980. His father, Jeremiah Jacob Stuart, replaced the three-over-three windows with one larger window, and his work caught on. By doing so, the watchman had a much better view, and many cabins throughout the state quickly changed their windows as well. Jeremiah lived to be 101. Richie painted the inside and replaced the floor. Two bunk beds were originally built for the watchmen. The cabin had a full kitchen with a gas stove and wood stove for heat. The bathroom was an outhouse. The porch was once screened in. In 1984, the Red Hill fire was reported by Richie. Chief James Hayes and Richie learned it had been set in six places. Several fires occurred on Belknap Mountain during the next few years. Richie had over 1,800 reports, and he was called "Hawkeye" by locals. (Courtesy of Susan Leach.)

MOUNT BELKNAP, GUNSTOCK MOUNTAIN, 1912. This is the view from Schoolhouse Hill Road. This mountain has quite a few names: Mount Belknap, Gunstock Mountain, or Mount Major. It is the most elevated and sits in the eastern part of town. It sits 2,384 feet in elevation. The carriage road, off Belknap Mountain Road, will bring one two-thirds of the way up to the highest peak. (Courtesy of Susan Leach.)

SCHOOLHOUSE HILL ROAD. This is the old road to the village, once the home of the first meetinghouse, called Schoolhouse Meetinghouse. This image of the side-by-side barns was made by well-known artist and photographer Loran Percy. Percy captured the beautiful old barns and road in one of his paintings. Prints were also made of his work. His art gallery was on Cherry Valley Road, just before Cat Path. Percy has captured quite a few of the scenic spots in town. Gunstock Recreational Area and the Gilford Public Library have some of his work on display as well as the town hall. His wife, Jane Percy, is one of Gilford's historians. (Courtesy of the Gilford Public Library.)

MT. BELKNAP, FROM GILFORD VILLAGE
ALTITUDE, 2400 FEET. OVERLOOKING LAKE WINNIPESAUKEE, N. H.

BRINGING THE BUGGY. Mount Belknap is seen in the background of this image, taken from Belknap Mountain Road in the horse-and-carriage era. The dirt road is a mass of wagon-wheel tracks, and one can see a single-horse wagon hitched to the fencing on the left. (Courtesy of the Thompson-Ames Historical Society.)

NORTH MAIN STREET. North Main Street is now Schoolhouse Hill Road. This is before Route 11A's intersection. On the left one can see the Morrill Farm; across on the right was the site of the first District 8 schoolhouse. (Courtesy of the Gilford Public Library.)

16

SOUTH MAIN STREET. Heading down what is now Belknap Mountain Road, on the left one can see the Sleeper-Sanborn home and the Union Meeting House. On the right are the Otto home and the Dolly Gilman home. (Courtesy of the Gilford Public Library.)

LACONIA AIRPORT. Laconia Airport is located on Route 11 in Gilford. The airport started out by being built for defense, but it was never used for that purpose. Car races once held here were called the Gilford Bowl. The airport covers 448 acres at an elevation of 545 feet, and there is one paved runway, over a mile long. In 1935, a grass strip became the first airport in Belknap County. Later, in 1941, the airport moved to the current location. Many improvements and renovations have happened over the years. The airport continues to be an important part of the community today. (Courtesy of Susan Leach.)

DAM ON GILFORD BROOK, ROUTE 11A. In 1937, there was a flood that took out a lot of the stonework at the dam. (Courtesy of Susan Leach.)

THE MEADOWBROOK BRIDGE, 1907. Today, the brook runs into the marina and onto Lake Winnipesaukee. Meadowbrook is one of six perennial brooks and streams located within Gilford. The others are Black Brook, Gunstock River, Jewett Brook, Poor Farm Brook, and West Alton Brook. The Harris Barn is on the right, which later became the Gilford Playhouse. The old brick farmhouse can still be seen today at the intersection of Route 11 and Route 11B. Kimball Castle is behind the branch on the elm tree, Locke's Hill Road. The train tracks ran in front of the playhouse back then. (Courtesy of Susan Leach.)

18

Two

COMMUNITY BUILDINGS
AND CELEBRATIONS

THE GILFORD VILLAGE STORE. The Gilford Village Store was originally opened in 1836 by Benjamin Jewett, Albert Chase, and Jeremiah Thing. Later, George W. Weeks and John Munsey worked together. Dr. Dearborn lived on the second floor and had an office. The Munseys added onto the store, and C.E. Merrill was next to run the business. It was then known as Wadley's Store and Grange Hall. Over the years, the store has had many storekeepers and owners. Each has added a little piece of themselves. Today, it remains the gathering spot of Gilford village, where locals stop in for a cup of coffee, a quick lunch, or the day's news. Children walk from the school for their favorite treats. On Gilford Old Home Day, there is no spot left unoccupied on its porch and roadside, as many gather there year after year. The gas pumps are gone, but the old wooden floorboards still creek as folks come and go. (Courtesy of Norm Soucy, Gilford Village Store.)

TOWN MEETING, 1920. The photographer captured this image standing on the town hall front lawn looking down Potter Hill Road, toward the Grange. On the left is the District 8 schoolhouse, which was originally a one-room school from 1892 to 1939. It then became the home of Ray Watson in 1940 and later the Whitney home in the 1950s. (Courtesy of Merrill Fay, Fay's Boatyard.)

THOMPSON-AMES UNION MEETINGHOUSE. The Union Meetinghouse Universalists occupied the Union Meetinghouse from 1834 through the 1850s. Pews were sold to pay for the construction of the building. That meant the family owned the pew and was guaranteed the same seating. No other family could use the pew. It stood vacant until the Methodist Episcopal Church came in 1874. In 1889, Gus Copp, owner of the Gunstock Brook sawmill, remodeled the building. He added the stained-glass windows, belfry, and domed alcove and painted the exterior. He also created the stunning hemlock wooden wall interior of the building that still exists today. (Courtesy of the Thompson-Ames Historical Society.)

THE GILFORD COMMUNITY CHURCH AND GILFORD TOWN HALL. This photograph shows off the Centennial Celebration Banner. The 100th anniversary program, dated June 17, 1912, had many songs, prayers, and recitations. It was an all-day celebration, with the last exercises commencing at 7:30 p.m. In 1970, the church was moved back and a steeple was added. Two decades later, the town hall was set back, and the two buildings were eventually joined. (Courtesy of Susan Leach.)

THE LAURA WEEKS HALL. Originally the site of the Free Will Baptist Church horse shed, the Laura Weeks Hall was built in 1938. Elizabeth Sanborn gave the hall in honor of Laura Ann Weeks, who lived on Gunstock Hill. The building was used for Sunday school classes, church day care, and also town offices. The first public works office; H. Richard Howarth's, the town's engineer, office; appraisal; the selectmen's office; and the department of land use were also in this building. Doris McHaffie was the secretary. (Courtesy of Susan Leach.)

EARLY TOWN HALL. Pictured here is the early town hall, which housed the town clerk, police, appraisal, and the selectmen's office, after these offices had been at Laura Weeks Hall. (Courtesy of Susan Leach.)

THE OLD LIBRARY. Built between 1924 and 1925, the land was donated by Rev. Wilbur Harding and his wife, Louisa Jane (Whitcomb) Harding. Labor was volunteered, and funds were appropriated by the town. (Courtesy of the Gilford Public Library.)

THE GRANGE. The Grange was built in 1857. Prior to becoming the Grange, it was a store and post office. It has belonged to the Thompson-Ames Historical Society since 1980. (Courtesy of the Thompson-Ames Historical Society.)

MILLER ESTATE. The is an early view of the Miller Estate, at what is known as Meadowbrook Farms. (Courtesy of Susan Leach.)

FREE WILL BAPTIST PARSONAGE. The parsonage was built approximately 1821 by Aram Smith, and a donation party was held here annually. Town folk brought and enjoyed whatever they had to share. After the party, extra food and supplies were shared with those less fortunate. (Courtesy of Susan Leach.)

THE METHODIST PARSONAGE. The Methodist parsonage was built in 1879. The home is believed to have been moved across the street from Deacon Hunter's property. The home was built for the Methodist church across the street, and the barn is actually older than the home. (Courtesy of Susan Leach.)

LAKES REGION PLAYHOUSE. Pictured here is a view of the Lakes Region Playhouse in the early years. Originally the Sanders Farm and later Spencer's Farm, the playhouse was open from 1947 until the 1960s. Mae West, Milton Berle, and Tallulah Bankhead were some of the entertainers that came to Gilford to perform. This was a premier location for many Hollywood stars to showcase their talents. (Courtesy of Susan Leach.)

SPRINGHOUSE AT LAKE VIEW PARK. Springhouses were used for refrigeration. The one-room buildings were constructed over a water source, usually a spring, which maintained cool temperatures year-round. (Courtesy of Susan Leach.)

LAKESHORE PARK. The Lakeshore Park was built for the employees and families of the Boston & Montreal Railroad. This building was used for entertainment and cooking. Many flocked to the park to enjoy their time off together with huge gatherings, cookouts, and parties. Families would bring along a tent to sleep beneath the huge pines. (Courtesy of Merrill Fay, Fay's Boatyard.)

GLENDALE STORE. This was a popular stop, adjacent to Lake Shore Road. It sat opposite what was once the Glendale Fire Station. Bent Mason (center) is standing on the porch. Mason was the owner in the mid-1920s and ran it until the late 1930s, when Irving Rand took over. It was then called Rand's Store. The building was eventually moved to Casey Road and belonged to Don Dockham for awhile in the 1960s and 1970s. (Courtesy of Merrill Fay, Fay's Boatyard.)

SAWYER'S DAIRY BAR. Sawyer's was the premier eating establishment in Gilford for a time. Pictured here is a typical evening with lots of patrons waiting for their number to be called. (Courtesy of Susan Leach.)

Alton Wilkes'
Lakes Region Playhouse
JUNCTION ROUTES 11 AND 11-B
LACONIA-GLENDALE, NEW HAMPSHIRE
TELEPHONE 293-4387

SCHEDULE OF PLAYS — 1966

WEEK OF	
July 4	KATHRYN (Mrs. Bing) CROSBY in "MARY, MARY" (4 year Broadway comedy hit)
July 11	CLIFF (Charlie Weaver) ARQUETTE in "YOU CAN'T TAKE IT WITH YOU" (Hilarious farce)
**July 15	2:30 p.m. Children's Show "PINOCCHIO" Ronor Marionettes
*July 18	(Pulitzer Prize Musical) "HOW TO SUCCEED IN BUSINESS WITHOUT REALLY TRYING" (Musical Comedy Laff Riot)
*July 25	SHEILA McCRAE in (Musical Hit) "GYPSY" (Miss McCrae will be seen all next season on TV with Jackie Gleason in the Honeymooners)
*Aug. 1	SHERRY BRITTON in "THE BEST OF BURLESQUE" (a nostalgic revival of an entertainment form once again sweeping the country—baggy pants comedians, chorus girls, and novelty (!) dancing (?) Miss Britton is a living doll!
*Aug. 8	(Smash English Musical) "OLIVER OLIVER" (2 yrs. in London - 2 yrs. on B'Way) Hit Song "As Long As He Needs Me"
Aug. 15	JUNE ALLYSON in "GOODBYE GHOST" (New play prior to B'Way) (This one is fun!)
**Aug. 16	2:30 p.m. Children's Show. "ALADDIN AND HIS MAGIC LAMP" Wizard Children's Production
Aug. 22	TOM EWELL in "THE IMPOSSIBLE YEARS" Play still playing on B'Way starring Allan King (Screams of Laughter)
Aug. 29	(B'Way & National Hit - Risque farce) "THE OWL & THE PUSSYCAT" Star to be announced.

— All Seats Reserved —

Eves. & Sat. Early Show	$3.00, $3.50, $3.90, $4.40
Wednesday Matinee	$2.30, $2.85, $3.30, $3.65
Saturday Late Show	$3.50, $3.95, $4.25, $4.50, $4.75

*Small increase in price this week.

CURTAIN TIMES
MONDAY through FRIDAY EVENINGS — 8:40
WEDNESDAY MATINEE — 2:30
Saturday Early Show—6:00.   Saturday Late Show—9:30
**Children's Show tickets, by reservation, $1.25
For Reservations and Season Tickets Call or Write Box Office

THE PLAYBILL. Lakes Region Playhouse was a summer theater that brought live performances to the area from 1950 to 1983. Bing Crosby, Groucho Marks, and Ginger Rogers were just a few of the performers at the playhouse. The playhouse could fit approximately 700 guests. Many local resident helped out on the day of the performances. The playhouse started to decline in ticket sales in the early 1960s. The barn was dismantled to move from the location but burned before it could be hauled away. (Courtesy of Susan Leach.)

GILFORD OLD HOME DAY, 1929. Pictured here is one of Gilford Old Home Day's floats in 1929. Note the two-horse team and the wagon driver's stovepipe hat. The budget for Gilford Old Home Day that year was $125. The selectmen were William Harris, John Hammond, and Clarence Henderson, and there were 127 horses in town that year. (Courtesy of Susan Leach.)

GILFORD CELEBRATING. Pictured here is a single-horse carriage in the Gilford Old Home Day parade. Notice which way the parade is traveling. It appears to be opposite of today's parades, perhaps because the town offices were not on Cherry Valley Road. Also notice the size of the girls' bicycle tires. (Courtesy of Susan Leach.)

EARLY CAR DECORATED FOR GILFORD OLD HOME DAY. The first automobile came to Gilford in 1910. Gilford farmers were not happy with the vehicles. They scared their horses, and the need to work on the roads only increased their taxes. It was not until 1925 that Gilford got gas pumps. (Courtesy of Susan Leach.)

AUGUST 23, 1929. The driver of this vehicle is Archie Andrews, and the four animals in the truck bed are the "Bremen Musicians" played by Dorothy Bean (cat), Walter Brock (dog), Lester Tilton (rooster), and Arthur Tilton (donkey). (Courtesy of the Thompson-Ames Historical Society.)

LIBERTY FLAG POLE DEDICATION, AUGUST 4, 1984. Pictured here are Louise Smith, Mrs. Kenneth Bonnette, Winifred Hackett, Donald Doblier Jr., Debbie Collette, Jennifer Lockwood, Karen Lockwood, Karen Phelps, Lisa Leach, Kim Rogers, and Sue Derby. On Gilford Old Home Day in 1976, the Gilford Bicentennial Commission held a tour of historic sites. A bronze plaque was placed at the Liberty Pole site. Funding came from the Thompson-Ames Historical Society, the Mary Butler Chapter, NDAR, and the Town of Gilford. Thomas T. Weekes reported that during the dedication, state officers of the Daughters of the American Revolution, Mary Butler Chapter regent, members of the board of selectmen, the mayor of Laconia, members of the Thomspon-Ames Historical Society, and members of the Gilford Village Historic District were all in attendance. (Courtesy of Susan Leach.)

Three

THE CASTLES OF GILFORD

KIMBALL'S CASTLE. Kimball's Castle was also known as the Broads. Benjamin Kimball purchased land from the Locke family in 1892, right above Belknap Point, on Locke's Hill. The land is the most elevated point on any Lake Winnipesaukee shore. It was after Kimball returned from Germany that he decided to build an exact replica of one of the castles he had visited on the Rhine River. He began building his masterpiece in 1894, and the castle was known as one of the finer summer homes, with one of the best 180-degree views in the Lakes Region. On either side of the doorway there were once two copper fish that caught the rainwater. The corners of the castle had gargoyles guarding the property. The castle had six chimneys but seven fireplaces, and the front door was three-inch-thick solid oak. The door knocker was a large lion's head. Hanging above the front door was a large wrought-iron lantern. Everything in the castle was thought out and done elegantly, with many items coming from all over by train. The oak and iron came from Europe. Many of the stones used to build the castle were taken right from the land on Locke's Hill. Italian masons were hired to work on the construction. (Courtesy of Susan Leach.)

KIMBALL'S CASTLE FROM BELNAP POINT

KIMBALL'S CASTLE HAUNTED. Sitting high upon Locke's Hill, this image features the view from Belknap Point. Over the years, there have been many stories passed down about strange noises and happenings at the castle. It was said that Myra Tilton Elliott Kimball was not as fond of the castle as her husband; however, she continued to use the castle after Benjamin had passed away. "An Ode to Kimball Castle," written by J.P. Polidoro, speaks to the landmark's plight: "Benjamin built me in 1879 to 1899—I am older than you / Italian stone-makers and laborers made me strong / The men were housed on the Lady of the Lake at the base of my land / She was moored there for them to reside, until my doors were opened / I am the Lady of Locke's Hill, as well / People have hiked me, they have skied me—that was the intent, now lost / in thicket and overgrowth, and shattered stone / Now you see me as cairn, a Joshua pile of stones, not a home, not a castle / Cairns guide you forward; You take me backwards / I still see the lake, the boats, and the mountains / Do not destroy me—I am still useful / I am a Castle, a Fortress, and I will not go easily into the night." (Courtesy of Susan Leach.)

CASTLE OVER LAKE WINNIPESAUKEE. Looking out from the castle, one can enjoy a magnificent view of Rattlesnake Island, Locke's, Welch, and Diamond Island as well as Governor's and Bear Island. All the activity on the lake with boats traveling back and forth must have been a joy to see. In 1906, Benjamin Kimball decided the castle needed a change, so he had white stucco applied to it. (Courtesy of Susan Leach.)

LOCATION. The Kimball's Castle property was located on approximately 280 acres of land known for its beauty. Carefully planted gardens, flower beds, and trimmed flowering trees were maintained and well kept. A large carriage house, groundskeeper quarters, a stable, and an icehouse were also included on the property. The castle is one of the properties in Gilford that is listed in the National Register of Historic Places. (Courtesy of Susan Leach.)

KIMBALL'S CASTLE NEGLECTED. The stone for the castle was brought by train from Concord, but most of the supply came from right at the construction site on Locke's Hill. There were steps all the way down to the lake, which was 800 feet below. In 1977, trustees of the castle offered the entire property to the Town of Gilford. The selectmen voted to accept in July 1978. In 1979, the town voted and accepted the property. The attorney general stipulated that the property can never be developed for residential, commercial, or industrial use. The town formed an association of Kimball Castle Trustees. During this time, the castle was opened for school classes and visitors. From that time to today, the castle has changed hands and purpose. Sadly neglected, it has been stripped of its grandeur and is a shell of what was once a rare jewel. (Courtesy of Susan Leach.)

THE BOLDUC FARM. The barn at Bolduc Farm was added in 1880. The farm became a stopping point for the Dover and Portsmouth mail route. People could change their horses there. The Bolduc family actually came in 1919, and they have continued the tradition of maple sugaring over the years. It takes 30 to 50 gallons of sap to make one gallon of maple syrup, and it takes a gallon of syrup to make eight pounds of maple candy. (Courtesy of the Bolduc family.)

THE SANBORN HOME. This home sits on Belknap Mountain Road. It was built by Henry Sleeper and Joseph Sanborn Jr. The wing on the house was moved from Lakeshore Road. The home was once known for blacksmithing, barrel making, and trading. (Courtesy of Susan Leach.)

THE SAMUEL GILMAN HOME. Pictured here are, from left to right, (seated on lawn) Ethel, unidentified, Ella Tracey Bailey, and Loren Stevens; (second row) Annie Parker, Dudley Parker, Sally Ann, Estelle Parker Tracy, and Bailey Freeman Parker. This is the original home of Samuel Gilman, currently owned by James Colby. (Courtesy of Susan Leach.)

THE KINGS GRANT INN. Also known as the Samuel Sanborn Farm, the Kings Grant Inn was built between 1813 and 1832. In the late 1800s, Matthew Kimball, Benjamin Kimball's cousin, bought the farm and opened it for summer visitors. William Vose bought the inn in the 1930s. As it was already set up for summer guests, they began to welcome winter skiers as well. In the 1950s, some of the performers who came to the Lakes Region Playhouse would hold parties and after show celebrations here. (Courtesy of Susan Leach.)

THE VICTORIAN HOUSE. This home was also known as the old Carr Tavern, the Stoddard House, and the Hampshire House. The land was originally purchased by James Elkins and Robert Carr in 1800, but the two separated the lots in 1812. Part of this land is known as Lake Shore Park. In 1823, two signs hung, one over the front door and one on the corner, that read: "Entertainment & Spirituous Liquors by R. Carr" and "R. Carr's Inn." The cost of an overnight stay with supper and breakfast for one man and two horses was $1. (Courtesy of Susan Leach.)

THE ENOCH HUNT HOME. Enoch Hunt came to the area in 1793, and his home was framed in 1795. Hunt married Sally Page, and they had 11 children. In 1812, the home was partially finished. William and Thomas Jefferson finished up the home. The ell was built in 1875 by Marshall Dexter. Work inside the house was done by Samuel P. Hunt, and the blinds were completed by Jeremiah Hunt. Local historian Carole Johnson grew up in this home. (Courtesy of Susan Leach.)

THE DIAMOND ISLAND HOUSE. This is the Diamond Island House, built in the 1860s. This photograph was used on the program for the 100th anniversary of the incorporation of Gilford. The island belonged to James Ames Jr., whose farm was not far away on the lakeshore. It was considered a great place to visit, stay, and dance. In the 1870s, the house was towed across the ice to its new home, in the Weirs, becoming the new Hotel Weirs. In 1924, it mysteriously burned. After the a hurricane in 1938, owner F. Carroll Spooner decided to sell the fallen trees from the island. He had them rolled into the lake and towed to Meredith for the Diamond Match Company. (Courtesy of Susan Leach.)

THE HUTCHINSON MANSION. This Governor's Island mansion was built in 1885. It was home to the founder and editor of the *Washington Post*. US presidents Grover Cleveland and Theodore Roosevelt and Amb. Count VonSternburg were said to have stayed at the mansion. (Courtesy of Susan Leach.)

AMES FAMILY FARM. The Ames Farm Inn has had five generations of family continue to run the business. The Ames family tree goes back to the descendants of one of the first families to settle in Gilford. David Ames built the farmhouse in the early 1800s, and James Noah Ames purchased the farm in 1891. James offered rooms and meals to visitors, and he built cottages along the shorefront. He also invited friends from Boston to build cottages on his 500-acre property. In addition, Ames Family Farm had its own railroad stop, which also brought guests. (Courtesy of the Ames Family Farm.)

THE RAND HOME. Located on Gunstock Hill Road, this was the home of R.W. Philbrick. Later, Andy Howe of Beans and Greens Farm lived here. (Courtesy of Susan Leach.)

THE ROWE HOUSE. This home was known as the Rowe House; Jesse Thing settled here in 1810. He had 86 acres and soon built a 1.5-story home. Benjamin Rowe bought the farm in 1815 and built the cape with bricks he made himself. He used sand from what was known as the Old Needham Pits, located at the junction of Routes 11A and 11B. Only six early brick capes have survived in Belknap County. The Rowe House is the only cape known in New Hampshire to have four interior chimneys. In 1835, Rowe joined the First Free Will Baptist Church and was elected ruling elder in 1837. Monthly meetings often were held at the farm. The farm's icehouse was moved to Easy Street and became Doc Hoyt's garden shed. Rowe's grandson Albanus died at the age of 15 of consumption. It was then that David Gould sold four acres, directly beside the Rowe House, for $25 to create a village cemetery, which came to be known as Pine Grove. Albanus was the first burial in the cemetery. His father, Simon, planted the row of red pines, which still stands today, to hide the grave from his wife's kitchen window. (Courtesy of the Thompson-Ames Historical Society.)

TRIPLE TROUBLE FARM. Pictured here is the Lake and Mountain House, located at 299 Cherry Valley Road, Route 11A. In the 1940s, Dr. William Smith grew blueberries at this farm as an experiment. Gilford actually had quite a few berry farms. The Curtis Farm had blueberries from 1941 to 1969. The High Maples Farm on Morrill Street had strawberries, peaches, and apples. (Courtesy of Susan Leach.)

Hampshire House

Located on a knoll with the Grand View of Lake Winnipesaukee and the White Mountains

Comfortable — Attractive — Clean — Restful

~

A reputation for real good home cooking

SANDY BATHING BEACH
         NEAR BELKNAP SKI AREA

~

ART and MILDRED NELSON
Route 11   —   Gilford-Laconia
     Telephone Glendale 2491
     Rates and Booklet on Request

THE HAMPSHIRE HOUSE. The Hampshire House is now known as the Victorian House. It is located on Route 11, just before the Ellacoya Country Store. Once owned by Art and Mildred Nelson, they described the home as being located on a knoll with a grand view of Lake Winnipesaukee and the White Mountains, comfortable, attractive, clean, and restful, with a reputation for good home cooking. The property featured a sandy bathing beach, near Belknap Ski Area, and their telephone number was Glendale 2491. (Courtesy of Susan Leach.)

THE WEEKS HOME. The farm sits on the corner of Belknap Mountain and Hoyt Roads. Hazen Weeks purchased the farm in 1832, and it has remained in the family ever since. The home is right next to what is known as the Under the Mountain Schoolhouse. (Courtesy of Peter Weeks, Weeks Farm Collection.)

GREYSTONE INN. Greystone overlooks the area on Lake Winnipesaukee known as the Broads. The view includes the White Mountains, and the inn has room for 50 guests. Located on Route 11 and Route 4, the inn was once run by Ralph V. Amsden and he placed an advertisement that proclaimed "A Vacation Paradise at Greystone Inn and Cabins." It boasted modern comforts, excellent cuisine, sports, amusements, shuffleboard, and croquet. It had its own 40-mile-per-hour speedboat. Reasonable rates offered accommodations for $4.50 and up daily and $28 and up weekly on the American Plan. Also, rooms and cabins were available on the European Plan. They prided themselves on hosting selected clientele and rural free delivery. Their telephone number was 4 Phone Glendale 2601. (Courtesy of Susan Leach.)

THE TILTON FARM. Originally the Thurston Farm and later the J.M. Ames Farm, the property is best known today as the Arthur Tilton Farm. The farm is located on Old Lake Shore Road. Arthur and his brother Lester grew up here on the farm. (Courtesy of Susan Leach.)

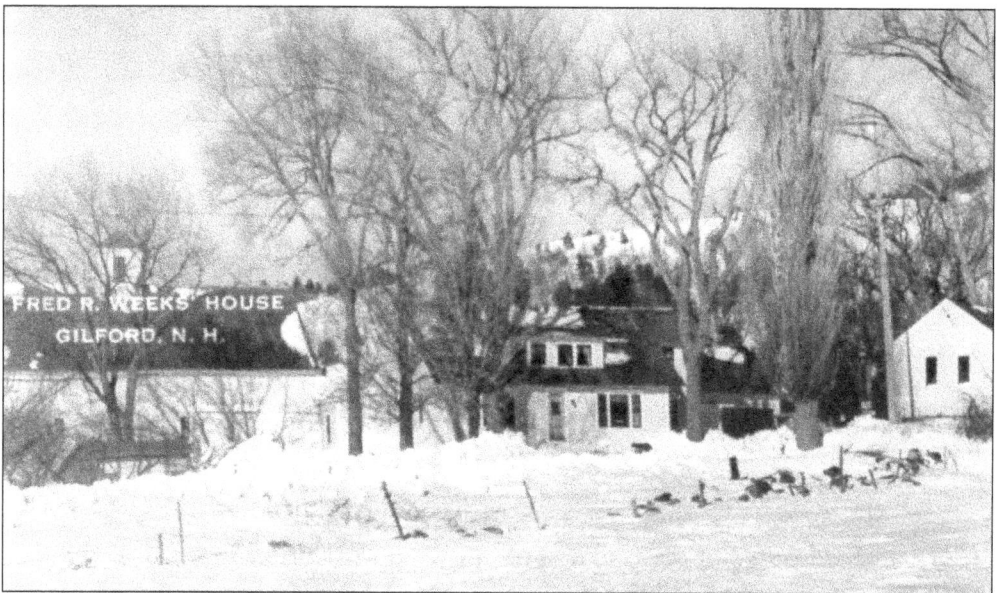

THE WEEKS FARM. Known as Weeks End Farm and Cabin, this farm offered lodging to those visiting the first tow rope in New Hampshire. Fred R. Weeks boasted 1,000-foot altitude at the foot of the Belknap Mountains and also let people know the farm was located near "the best ski jump in the United States." (Courtesy of Peter Weeks, Weeks Farm Collection.)

Four

HORSES, CARRIAGES, AND THE FARM

THE GILFORD HEARSE. Once belonging to Gilford, this hearse carried loved ones to neighborhood cemeteries such as Hoyt and Weeks Cemetery. It was sold at auction and lovingly restored by the Mayhew Funeral Home in Meredith, New Hampshire. (Courtesy of the Mayhew Funeral Home and Susan Leach.)

GILFORD OLD HOME DAY, AUGUST 23, 1929. The driver is Arthur LaBonte, and the little boy next to him is his son Leo "Pete" LaBonte. The LaBonte family owned and ran Mountain View Farm on Hoyt Road. The farm was well known for milk deliveries and haying many of Gilford's fields. Pete was an active member in the Thompson-Ames Historical Society, giving talks on how the old dairy farms were maintained and managed. He also worked for Gilford's public works department, plowing the roads of Gilford for many years. He will be remembered for his contagious laugh, smile, and love of days gone by in Gilford. (Courtesy of the LaBonte Family Farm Collection, Dottie LaBonte.)

FRANK AND WALKER BACON. This is the early 1930s, but the first Gilford Old Home Day was in 1919. It was originally held on a Thursday. Early Gilford Old Home Days were under the Grange master's leadership. The Grange became heavily involved. The parade became an annual tradition beginning in the early 1930s. (Courtesy of the Thompson-Ames Historical Society.)

GILFORD FIRE DEPARTMENT WAGON. A fire wagon arrived in Gilford in 1914. It was pulled by horses. There were 215 horses, 6 mules, 30 oxen, and 385 cows in town at the time. (Courtesy of Gilford Fire Rescue.)

EARLY 1900S. In the morning on Gilford Old Home Day, the organizers held a baseball game. They had a greased-pig race and a greased-pole event. Lunch was a baked bean dinner in the Grange hall, or a picnic behind the town sheds on Potter Hill Road under the pines. In the afternoon, a speaker would be in the town hall. The evening event was held at the Grange, usually a play or dance. (Courtesy of Susan Leach.)

GILFORD WHITE HORSE CARRIAGE. This family was dressed for a special day. Notice the stovepipe hat, shawl, fancy dress, and full suit. Most people had one set of Sunday-best clothes, while the remaining pieces in their wardrobe were for farm work. (Courtesy of Susan Leach.)

TRAVELING IN TOWN. Many people came into town with whatever they had for transportation. Wagons and buggies were common. This beautiful wagon shows an excellent example of the old wagon wheels. American wagon wheels are like no other wagon wheels in the world; creating a good wheel is a labor-intensive enterprise. Good wheels are made by wheelwrights who have many years of experience. Wheelwrights are a cross between carpenters and blacksmiths. Hickory wood makes the best wheel, though some are made of oak and ash. (Courtesy of Susan Leach.)

TWO-HORSE HITCH. Raising poultry was popular at the farms in town. Goose and turkey all made an appearance from time to time. Horses were kept, not for profit, but for working, convenience, and completing the barnyard. Some small business was done to bring horses to market or to sell. Horse power was needed for transportation—stagecoaches, wagons, and buckboards. Later, the Posh Club became popular in Gilford. People would spend many hours cleaning and brushing their horses for shows and parades. Oxen were also trained for the heavy field and tree work. Horses and oxen remain prevalent in the town today. (Courtesy of Susan Leach.)

EARLY AUTOMOBILE. The first automobile came to Gilford in 1910. The farmers were not exactly impressed with the noise they made because it frightened the horses. They were also upset because fixing the roads for automobiles raised their taxes. It was not until 1912 that more automobiles came to town. (Courtesy of Susan Leach.)

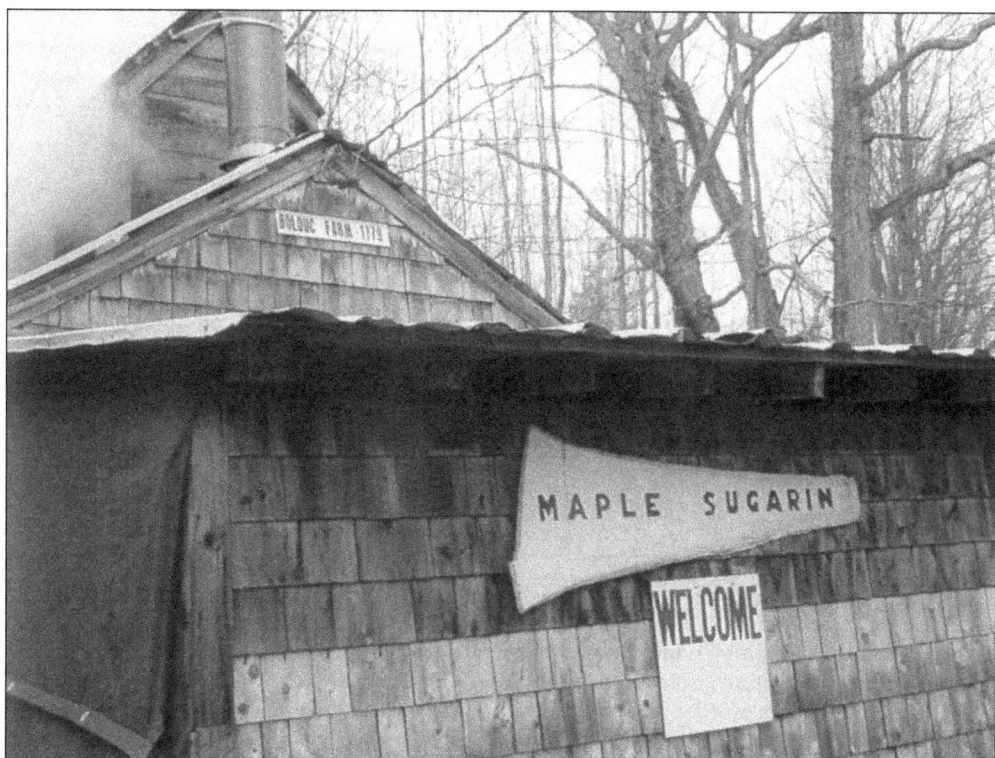

THE BOLDUC FARM. The family originally came down from Canada, but Armond, Ernie, and Hector's mother was born in Gilford in 1917. The Bolduc Farm, at 500 Morrill Street, has been producing maple syrup since 1779. It is the oldest continuous maple syrup operation in the country. Benjamin Jewett purchased 40 acres from Ebenezer Smith in March 1789. He built a small home on the property, which still stands as a shed today. The large home was built around 1838 and had to be remodeled after a lightning strike in 1880. The Bolducs purchased the farm in 1919. (Courtesy of the Bolduc Farm.)

THE BOLDUC BROTHERS. Yes, all brothers have been active members in both Gilford and Laconia by speaking to the public about history. Father Bolduc, who is no longer with us, along with his brothers, attended many historical society functions to speak on subjects varying from milk bottles, dairy production, and maple syrup production to the old town farms and many more. The Bolduc brothers came forward during the bicentennial and created Gilford's bicentennial collectors medallion. All have been active members serving on various committees in both Gilford and Laconia. Father Bolduc also wrote a book on the history of Gilford. The list goes on and on of all the various things these three gentlemen have done to promote and save parts of Gilford's past. (Courtesy of the Bolduc Farm.)

THE HERD. The Bolduc Farm is well known for its herd of buffalo, originally from Yellowstone National Park; burros from Death Valley; and white-faced Herefords. (Courtesy of the Bolduc Farm.)

SUGARING. Many friends and relatives look forward to maple sugar season on Bolduc Farm. Here, Sheldon Morgan checks the depth of the sap-holding tanks. (Courtesy of the Bolduc Farm.)

BLUEBERRIES. Gilford once produced large crops of blueberries. People were hired seasonally to hand pick the berries, which covered the back of Gunstock Mountain. Today, many bushes still blanket the mountain, but bears and wildlife now feast on the sweet berries. (Courtesy of Susan Leach.)

THE KINGS GRANT INN. Samuel Sanborn purchased 40 acres on what is now known as Kimball Road in June 1813. By 1832, he had built a homestead, stable, and shed. Matthew Kimball, a cousin of Benjamin Kimball, bought the farm and remodeled it. He opened it to summer tourists in the late 1800s. Later, William Vose took over and continued to take in boarders. (Courtesy of Susan Leach.)

THE BATES HOME. Frank "Pa" Bates's home was on the left heading down to the town docks. He was very well known at the docks. He sold bait and gasoline and also had a boat taxi service. Bates was known for wearing a hearing aid, always having an extra battery handy in his pocket. His boat was known as the *Mary Jane*. It ran only half of the time and had to be towed into dock on more than one occasion. (Courtesy of Frank Bates and Merrill Fay, Fay's Boatyard.)

TILTON FARM. Arthur Tilton and his calf are pictured here on the farm, at 264 Old Lake Shore Road. Tilton grew up in Gilford and was an active member of the community. He became one of Gilford's historians later in life. The farm was known for shipping apples as far away as England in the early 1900s. Tilton protected much of the farm with conservation easements. (Courtesy of Merrill Fay, Fay's Boatyard.)

THE GRANT FARM. Andrew purchased 200 acres in an area of town known as Back of the Mountain in 1792. In 1817, the farm sold to John Eaton. The Eatons were the next family to live at the farm in 1845. Levi Grant purchased the farm, and it remained in his family for many years. The cemetery on the property is known as Grant Cemetery and cannot be seen from the road.

Burials in the cemetery go back to the early 1880s. The woman pictured here is Villie Grant. She was born, lived, and died in this home at age 88. The home burned due to a faulty stove. Also pictured here is the milk room with Belknap and Gunstock Mountains keeping watch. Note the rain barrel, bundles of shakes, and the giant wood pile. (Courtesy of Susan Leach.)

HISTORIC FARM. Ames Family Farm sits on 135 acres with a quarter mile of sandy beach. The farm is now run by the fourth and fifth generation of family here in Gilford. Today, the inn has a variety of different lodging choices, from rooms in the main lodge to individual cabins. Breakfast at the inn offers daily specials, and it is well-known for serving fresh blueberry pancakes with New Hampshire maple syrup. (Courtesy of the Ames Family Farm.)

FRANKLIN D. POTTS, 1912. This home had one of the first artesian wells in Gilford. Franklin Potts named it Windover, and the house was destroyed by fire in the 1960s. (Courtesy of Susan Leach.)

SAWYER'S. Sawyer's Farm is located on Route 11B in the Intervale. Years ago, the Intervale was the part of town from Old Lake Shore Road, 11B, to the junction of 11A. Now the Intervale includes the airport and Sawyer's Meadow. Ebenezer Smith originally owned the farm and died in 1831. He died after being thrown from a wagon. Ebenezer's son John "Squire" Smith took over after his father's death. In the 1870s, John J. Morrill purchased the farm. Later, John's son John B. Morrill took over and raised cattle. It was not long after the farm became one of Gilford's largest dairy farms that Ansel and Ernest Sawyer bought the enterprise. (Courtesy of Susan Leach.)

THE BROWN FARM. Later known as the Alberg on Cherry Valley Road and once located at the entrance to Gunstock Mountain Resort, this farm became a sports shop with equipment, clothing, and supplies for a fun day at the mountain. The Alberg was taken down and removed in 2014. (Courtesy of Susan Leach.)

MOUNT BELKNAP FARM, 1916. The farm belonged to Leon Morrill before Bert Wadleigh purchased the property. The road to the fire tower on Mount Belknap is in back of the house. (Courtesy of Susan Leach.)

MEADOWBROOK FARM, 1873. This image can be seen at the Thompson-Ames Historical Society. In 1818, Joseph Potter owned the farm, and his son was the next owner. In 1823, Jonathan Thompson had the farm and later George Sanders owned it. The Davis family allowed visitors and neighbors who were Baptists to build cottages on the property in the late 1800s. (Courtesy of the Thompson-Ames Historical Society.)

BARN RAISING. A raising bee was often needed to build the big barns. The neighbors and community people would gather at the site for the raising. Many would bring food to share at mealtime. (Courtesy of Susan Leach.)

THE ROWE HOUSE. Pictured is the 1838 Rowe House, also known as the Wilson Farm. Here, Alvah D. Wilson and his wife, Ruth Edna (Sawyer) Wilson are standing out in the front of the farm. They were married on January 31, 1930. Originally, Jesse Thing owned the farm here, which included 86 acres. This home is now owned by the Town of Gilford and rented by the Thompson-Ames Historical Society. All that remains is the cape home. (Courtesy of the Thompson-Ames Historical Society.)

HARVEY RAND WITH HEREFORD. The barn here is now on the opposite side of Route 11B, Intervale Road, in Gilford. In 1995, the barn became Beans and Greens Farm, owned and managed by Martina and Andy Howe. (Courtesy of Susan Leach.)

OX-K FARM. No Gilford Old Home Day would be complete without a team of oxen. It is a tradition that has been in Gilford for generations. Each year, Ron and Kathy Salanitro from Ox-K Farm on Belknap Mountain Road bring their boys down to the town hall and patiently wait to end the parade with the yoked teams. People have enjoyed meeting and learning about the ox teams for many years, as the Salanitros are known for making special appearances at many events and locations held in town. Kathy Salanitro was also named Mrs. Senior New Hampshire in 2013. (Courtesy of Ox-K Farm.)

Five

BOATING AND
THE LAKESHORES

THE MOUNT WASHINGTON STEAMER. Although this steamer was built in Alton Bay in 1872, the first steamboat on Lake Winnipesaukee was built in 1832 in Lake Village. Here, the *Mount Washington* is pulling into Glendale. At 178 feet long, the steamer was one of the larger boats to frequent Glendale at that time. (Courtesy of Merrill Fay, Fay's Boatyard.)

STEAMER AT DOCK, C. 1910. The travelers on the *Governor Endicott* are heading into Ames Family Farm to board the Lake Shore Railroad. Ames was a popular spot to board the train as well as boats heading out to different spots on Lake Winnipesaukee. Ames Family Farm had its own train stop on the Lake Shore rail line. Visitors could set the farm as their destination and have everything in one stop. With clean boarding, plenty of food and ice, and the lovely shore of Lake Winnipesaukee, travelers were pleased to spend their vacations onsite. With plenty of

vegetables and baked goods on hand, the farm was known for delicious meals. In 1908, the Ames family had two boats to take people around the lake. Some travelers made Ames a stop along the way to upper parts of the lake. Eventually, the train station was moved across the road and made into one of the cottages. Lake-cut ice was still in use until the 1940s. Summers now at the farm are still busy, with vacationers yearning for that relaxing lakefront experience while indulging in some of the best-cooked meals on the lake. (Courtesy of the Ames Family Farm.)

BELOVED GLENDALE. This is the Glendale Dock long before the pavement. (Courtesy of Merrill Fay, Fay's Boatyard.)

THE STEAMER. The *Mount Washington* steamer is coming into dock at Glendale. (Courtesy of Merrill Fay, Fay's Boatyard.)

THE TOWN DOCKS, 1924. The public wharf at Glendale is pictured here before the enlargement of the launch and dock area. This is during the wooden-boat era, long before the fiberglass boats of today. The beautiful Ossipee Mountain Range can be seen in the background. (Courtesy of Merrill Fay, Fay's Boatyard.)

MAILBOXES. Glendale has long been known for the line of mailboxes that service those with island homes. This photograph shows summer folk waiting to pick up their mail at Glendale. There are 21 Winnipesaukee Islands in Gilford. Diamond, Governor's, Locke's, Mark, Timber, and Welch are the largest. (Courtesy of Susan Leach.)

THE GOSS STORE. Step inside the Noah Goss Store located at the Glendale town docks. This little general store was in business for many years during the Lake Shore Railroad era. This photograph was taken in the early 1900s. The railroad station was located to the right of the store. Passengers could stop and pick up supplies before heading to the lake. In the early times, the building was used to store ice. Goss sold the store to Clarence Henderson, who ran the store for years. During that time, Glendale was known as Henersey's Landing. Later, the store became Dorothy's Kitchen and then Gretchen's. Today, it is home of the Lion's Den, a favorite for both locals and visitors. The outdoor porch with stunning views is now enclosed. The wonderful smell from the kitchen surrounds the area, and most days the restaurant is full of people enjoying its fine cuisine. (Courtesy of Susan Leach.)

SMITH COVE. Smith Cove, on Lake Winnipesaukee, is pictured here. In the background, one can see the old icehouse where ice was stored for summer use. (Courtesy of Merrill Fay, Fay's Boatyard.)

DOCK ROAD, KINGS GRANT. This is Dock Road heading down to the water at Glendale. It also shows what is called a king's grant, which means the right-of-way. (Courtesy of Susan Leach.)

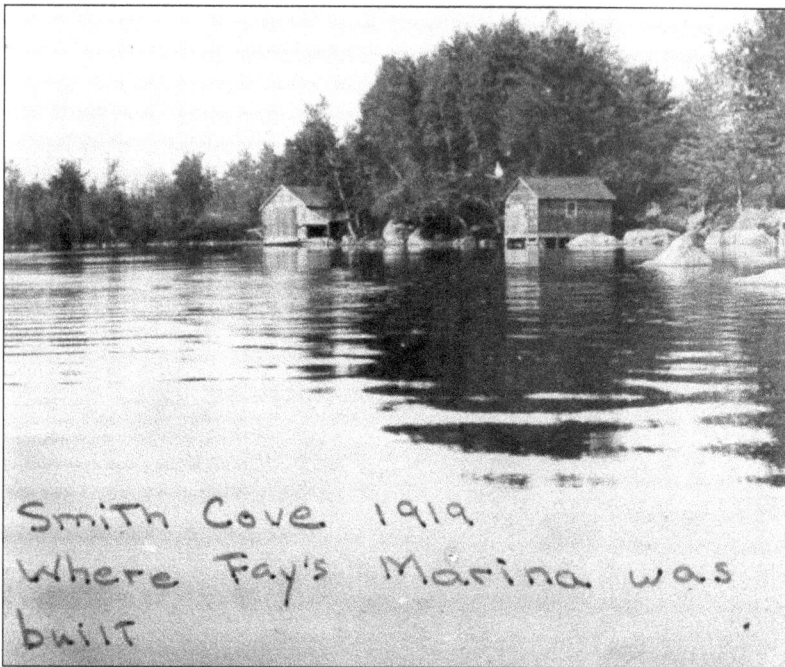

LOOKING BACK. Smith Cove is pictured here in 1919. This is where Fay's Boatyard is today. (Courtesy of Merrill Fay, Fay's Boatyard.)

Smith Cove 1919
Where Fay's Marina was
built

HENDERSON'S. Glendale Boathouse was built by Clarence Henderson about 1930. Henderson was noted for being one of Gilford's best selectmen. This location is the precursor to the future Glendale Boatyard. (Courtesy of Shirley Burns.)

GLENDALE COMPLEX. Pictured here is the Goss Store as well as the railroad station, tracks, and boatyard. Goss was station master, and he and his wife also ran the store, with the icehouse below. (Courtesy of Shirley Burns.)

LAKE SHORE PARK. In 1936, Lake Shore Park was listed as being on Route 4. The park advertised cabins to accommodate 150 people. Rates were $10 to $15 per week, and camping for 400 tents was available. Swimming, fishing, and bowling were common leisure activities enjoyed by visitors. (Courtesy of Lake Shore, Susan Leach.)

CASTLE AND SMITH COVE, 1916. Pictured here is Kimball's Castle at the very top of Locke's Hill. The next building down at center is Frank "Pa" Bates House, at Glendale. To the right of the Bates home is the Glendale Railroad Station. One can just barely make out the railroad tracks to the right of the station. On the shoreline at right is the Roberts/Petrino home. The boathouse was taken down after neighbors petitioned to have it removed. (Courtesy of Merrill Fay, Fay's Boatyard.)

MERRILL FAY'S BOAT, FAY'S BOATYARD. The boat on the left is a 23-foot-long 1947 Chris Craft, and the boat on the right is a 26-foot-long 1947 Holiday Steelcraft, Model No. 1777. In September 1954, Hurricane Carol hit Gilford. Merrill Fay was just a teenager when he headed out in the powerful Steelcraft boat to bring supplies to some of his relatives on Bear Island. He had not heard from them. The winds were 80 miles per hour, and the waves were 15 feet high with 100 feet or more between crests. He tried to make the lee of Timber Island but had to return to Smith Cove until the storm weakened. (Courtesy of Merrill Fay, Fay's Boatyard.)

JOHN GOODHUE SR. HAVING FUN OUT ON LAKE WINNIPESAUKEE. In 1957, Capt. John Goodhue had completed dredging two lagoons, one 700 feet long by 800 feet wide and the other 400 feet by 110 feet. He estimated 30,000 boat registrations then, with one-third of them on Lake Winnipesaukee. (Courtesy of the Goodhue family.)

GOODHUE BOATYARD. The Goodhues have ties on Lake Winnipesaukee that go back to the steamboat days in 1844. The yard was extremely busy throughout the 1950s. During the wooden-boat era, maintenance was much higher than the fiberglass boats of today. Carpenters and paint crews were always on hand. The yard had five boats that served as taxis back and forth from the islands. It was mostly a repair, service, and storage facility, but the boatyard also sold gasoline. The boatyard burned in 1960 on Halloween night. It was rebuilt, but Goodhue sold many of his properties around the lake to help finance the project. (Courtesy of the Goodhue family.)

GOODHUE'S. John "Jack" Goodhue and the crew at the boatyard stopped to gather for this photograph. (Courtesy of the Goodhue family.)

COLBY'S. Pictured here Colby's bathing beach at Smith Cove. Many people recall the days of the wooden boats, long before the fiberglass boats of today. Many of these boats were used as the first taxis back and forth to island homes. (Courtesy of Susan Leach.)

DELIVERING THE MAIL, 1957. These mailboxes are the island dwellers' main point of contact with the mainland. (Courtesy of Merrill Fay, Fay's Boatyard.)

FAY'S BOATYARD. Wilbur and Hazel Fay started the boatyard in 1944. Wilbur died in 1959, and his son Merrill returned from Michigan State to take over the boatyard. Merrill still works there today. (Courtesy of Merrill Fay, Fay's Boatyard.)

FAY'S BOATYARD. Fay's is an eight-acre boatyard that was established in 1944, located in Smith's Cove. Known as a complete marine facility, it employs factory-trained mechanics knowledgeable in all aspects of marine engines. They are professionals in sailing, offering complete rigging and retrofitting. (Courtesy of Merrill Fay, Fay's Boatyard.)

HENDERSON BOATYARD. Before the yard was Goodhue's and Francis, Clarence Henderson owned the Henderson Boatyard (also known as the Glendale Boatyard and McDuffy Marine). Insurance, inspections, and engine and hull repairs were available. Henderson was known as a walking bank; if anyone needed to cash a check, they would see him. He always carried a lot of cash and a pistol. (Courtesy of Shirley Burns.)

AMES FAMILY FARM. David Ames invited Boston friends to build cottages on the farm and added matching cottages along the shore. (Courtesy of the Ames Family Farm.)

Bathing Beach, Ames Farm, RFD 4, Lake Winnipesaukee, N. H.

AMES FAMILY FARM BEACHFRONT. Ames family members still run the historic Ames Farm Inn, offering lodging and delicious meals. (Courtesy of the Ames Family Farm.)

Six

LAKE SHORE RAILROAD

LAKE SHORE RAILROAD LOCOMOTIVE. Tuesday, June 17, 1890, was opening day for the Lake Shore Railroad. The announcement stated, "Three hundred speakers, each limited to talk three weeks. Two hundred locomotives, dressed in paper collars and stove pipe hats, will haul the trains of thought for the speakers. The longest words will be hauled on log trains. Tables will be set the length of the road on both sides." (Courtesy of Merrill Fay, Fay's Boatyard.)

1745- B.&M.R.R. Sta., Belknap Point, NH

GILFORD STATION. George Sanders had a farm at the Intervale. When the railroad line was built, it cut his property in two. The Lake Shore Railroad gave him a land-damage settlement, but Sanders was not happy with the settlement, so a group of lawyers, officials, and newspaper reporters climbed aboard a train in Lakeport and rode through the line. It was decided the settlement was adequate, so Sanders built a train stop, and Joe Sanders became stationmaster. The Gilford stops along the railroad gave people an option for travel. It was sometimes easier to hop on the train rather than hitch up the horses. Children also used the train to get to school. Island residents used the train to travel or shop and then returned to the docks. The Gilford Station still stands today, as a private home. (Courtesy of Merrill Fay, Fay's Boatyard.)

Winter at Glendale
Tracks along shore of Winnepesaukee

WINTER TRACKS. Winter on the railroad could be a problem for the railroad's operating department. Sometimes they would have to combine locomotives to make high grades. Crews also had to be on hand to dig out snow- and ice-clogged switches. (Courtesy of Susan Leach.)

THE MILLER FAMILY, 1910. A Lake Shore Railroad whistle stop was located behind what is now Patrick's Pub. There were a few stops along the tracks that were not enclosed. People would flag down the train if they wanted to be picked up. (Courtesy of Susan Leach.)

LAKESHORE PARK DEPOT. The depot is one of the buildings that has survived time. It has had a number of changes over the years. Originally wide open, it was later enclosed. It has been a restaurant, motel, and telegraph office operated by Harriet Sargent, the first woman telegrapher in New Hampshire. (Courtesy of Lakeshore Park.)

GLENDALE. Goss was station master, and he and his wife ran both the store and icehouse at Glendale. (Courtesy of Shirley Burns.)

STEAM TRAIN, NO.122, 1897. Train No. 122 is pictured here at the Glendale Train Station. The railroad ended service in 1930, and the tracks were dismantled in 1933. (Courtesy of Merrill Fay, Fay's Boatyard.)

LAKESHORE PARK. Lakeshore Park opened on June 26, 1891, and the park's popularity brought an increased number of passengers to the railroad. There was a grand ball held to celebrate the park's opening. (Courtesy of Lakeshore Park.)

GLENDALE STATION. The Glendale Station was the next stop after Meadowbrook Station aboard the Lake Shore Railroad. This station brought many summer visitors to the boat docks and became the center of attention in Glendale. The railroad station helped boost the demand for ice cut from Lake Winnipesaukee. (Courtesy of Susan Leach.)

JANUARY 25, 1923. It took 40 years to complete the railroad. In 1934, the number of passengers had decreased, as well as the amount freight being shipped. An application for abandonment of the rail was approved on May 25, 1935. (Courtesy of Merrill Fay, Fay's Boatyard.)

Seven

SKIING AND LODGING

FRED R. WEEKS END CABIN AND HOUSE. The Weeks family has lived on Weeks Road generation after generation. (Courtesy of Peter Weeks, Weeks Farm Collection.)

DINAN FAMILY PHOTOGRAPH. James Henry Dinan and his wife, Bertina, are pictured here on their 1947 chrome Indian Chief. They are at the Belknap Recreational Area, which was once home to the Rally's Races and the popular Hill Climb in later years. (Courtesy of the Dinan family.)

BARAKS LODGE. The Baraks was a place for skiers to lodge, known as snug bunking. Built by Harry Sleeper, the house could fit 72 skiers in bunk beds. There was a fireplace and pool table. (Courtesy of the Gunstock Family Inn.)

BARAKS ADVERTISEMENT. The Baraks was affordable, fun, and a place for skiers to gather after a full day of skiing. Many stories were swapped around the fireplace of the day's adventures. (Courtesy of the Gunstock Family Inn.)

BARAKS FIREPLACE. The stone fireplace was not only a good place to gather, it also helped dry all the wet clothing. Many cords of wood would be burned during the winter season. (Courtesy of the Gunstock Family Inn.)

SLEEPING IN THE BARAKS. Pictured here is one of the eight rooms with double bunk beds. There were also rooms with many single bunk beds. (Courtesy of the Gunstock Family Inn.)

INSIDE OF THE BARAKS. The inside was lined with knotty pine boards, which created a lodge-type feeling. (Courtesy of the Gunstock Family Inn.)

BULLDOZER. During renovations to the Baraks, the giant stone chimney was removed from the front of the building. (Courtesy of the Gunstock Family Inn.)

GUNSTOCK INN. A massive renovation and addition was completed to create the Gunstock Inn. (Courtesy of the Gunstock Family Inn.)

SCENIC VIEWS. The decks at Gunstock Inn provided a beautiful view of the mountains and the lake. (Courtesy of the Gunstock Family Inn.)

NEW SIGNAGE. Pictured here is the new Gunstock Acres sign being installed. The mid-1960s brought about the largest development in the state. Gunstock Acres consisted of 800 acres on a steep mountain side across from the Gunstock Ski Area, and 776 house lots were laid out. (Courtesy of the Gunstock Family Inn.)

BELKNAP RECREATIONAL AREA. The Belknap Recreational Area was a project of the Works Progress Administration (WPA). The main lodge was built from wood cut right in the area, and granite from Cobble Mountain was used. It officially opened February 28, 1937. (Courtesy of the Gunstock Recreational Area.)

GUNSTOCK LODGE. Built during the Great Depression, the lodge was mostly constructed from onsite materials. This was not always a frugal measure, but it created work to help through that era. Lumber was cut onsite and hauled by horses. The large oak timbers can still be seen in the lodge today. The granite or stone was also taken onsite. It was heated by a very large stone fireplace in the main hall. The fireplace still adds warmth to the hall and also serves as a place for people to enjoy the crackle and blaze while grabbing a bite to eat. The balcony creaks as one walks across the old floorboards, gazing down to the lower floor. The lodge has seen thousands of visitors, skiers, snowboarders, campers, and hikers. Hundreds of wedding receptions and special parties have been held within the walls, even some sad times with memorial services as well. It is maintained by the Gunstock staff, painted, scrubbed, and repaired each day. Generation after generation return year-round, participating in all the events the old lodge holds. (Courtesy of the Gunstock Recreational Area.)

GUNSTOCK SKI SCHOOL. Olympian Penny Pitou and her husband, Egon Zimmerman, opened up the Penny Pitou Ski School at Gunstock Recreational Area in the 1960s. They opened this school after the Squaw Valley Olympics. The school included schoolchildren and clubs as well as ski instruction for the disabled. Others that also coached and taught were Gary Allen and Klaus Buttinger. (Courtesy of the Gunstock Recreational Area.)

LIFT. The first lift was known as a banana hanger, and it was the first chairlift in the East. It came to the Belknap Recreation Area in 1938. The next lift was a single chair. (Courtesy of the Gunstock Recreational Area.)

SKI TRAILS OF GUNSTOCK. The first slopes opened were Fletcher Hale and Stonebar in 1936. Phelps and Smith came in 1937. The following year brought Try Me, and Tiger was next. Red Hat, named after Fritzie Baer, who always wore a red hat, came after Tiger. Tiger, Gunsmoke, Recoil, and Hot Shot in the Pistol Area came when Warren Warner brought in two double-chair lifts. (Courtesy of the Gunstock Recreational Area.)

Penelope Theresa "Penny" Pitou won silver medals in the 1960 Olympics' downhill event, placing second in both downhill and giant slalom. Penny learned to ski first in her own backyard and then at the Gilford Outing Club. Later, she practiced at Belknap Mountain (now Gunstock) Ski Area. Penny went to Laconia High School, and there she tried out for the ski team, although there was a no girls allowed rule. She made the team, tucking her hair up into her hat. She was inducted to the New England Women's Sports Hall of Fame. She married Egon Zimmermann, Olympic gold medalist and World Cup alpine ski racer. (Courtesy of Susan Leach.)

Skiing on Phelps Open Slope, Belknap Mountains Recreation Area
Gilford, N. H.

PHELPS SLOPE. This is Phelps in 1942. The lift was the second added for the 1938–1939 season. (Courtesy of the Gunstock Recreational Area.)

Eight

GILFORD SCHOOLING

SUNDAY SCHOOL CLASS. This class is standing on the stairs of the Laura Weeks Hall, also known as Maple Rest. Some of the children included in the photograph are David Blanford, Martha Cram, William Morrill, Jennifer Smith, Bonnie McCaffie, Elinor Smith, Peter Weeks, Sandra Clifford, Reed Wallace, Mary Helen Curits, and Bill Littlefield Jr. (Courtesy of Susan Leach.)

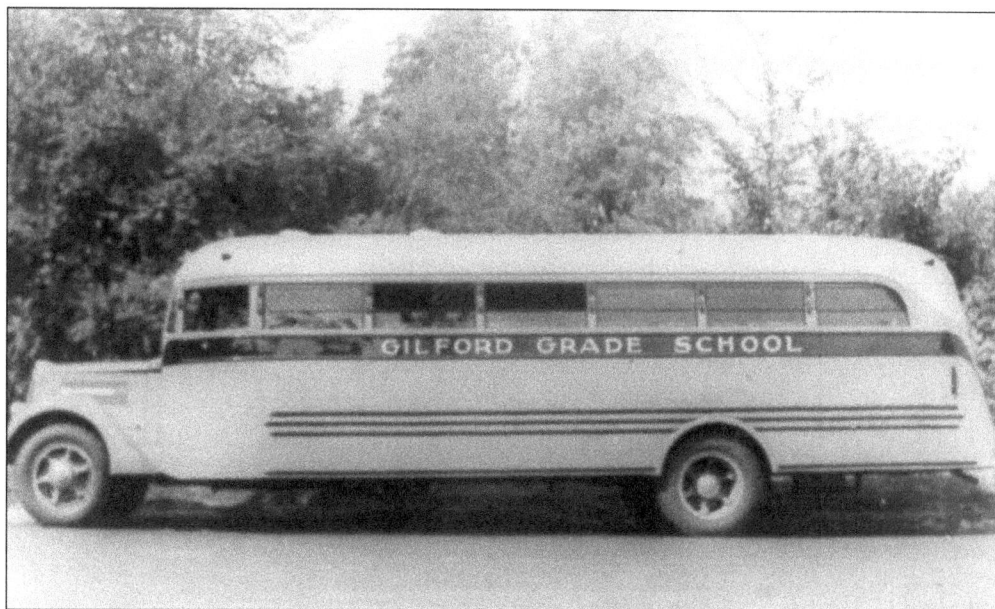

GILFORD'S FIRST BUS. Prior to Gilford getting a bus, children had to walk or find any way possible to get to school. Some neighborhoods would gather children with a buckboard or wagon, and some children would catch a ride aboard the train when the railroad opened. (Courtesy of Susan Leach.)

ONE-ROOM SCHOOLS. The school districts in 1872 were Intervale, Carrs, Mooneys, Laconia, Thyngs, Pond, White Oaks, Gilford Village, Under the Mountains, Liberty Hill, Back of the Mountain, Morrills, Lake Village, and Dames. This is a class photograph of the Lily Pond School from about 1930. (Courtesy of Susan Leach.)

GOVERNOR'S ISLAND SCHOOLHOUSE. Originally located on the corner of Summit Avenue and Weirs Road, this schoolhouse was moved down the road and later taken down. (Courtesy of Susan Leach.)

HOYT ROAD SCHOOLHOUSE, NO. 9. Pictured here around 1930, the Mountain School is located across from the Weeks Cemetery, next to the farm owned by Ben Weeks and his wife, Mildred Weeks. It was also known as the Weeks School. This is one of the few remaining schoolhouses intact. (Courtesy of Susan Leach.)

Nine

GILFORD TOWN FOLK

THE BEAN FAMILY. This is a Bean family photograph. The Bean family has lived in Gilford for multiple generations, and many members now reside in homes on Saltmarsh Pond Road. (Courtesy of the Bean family.)

WILLIAM STARK WEEKS, 1873–1935. This photograph was taken on August 23, 1929. Weeks was ballot inspector in 1929, given $9 by the town. (Courtesy of Peter Weeks, Weeks Farm Collection.)

STARK WEEKS. This photograph was part of Mildred Weeks photo album. (Courtesy of Peter Weeks, Weeks Farm Collection.)

96

WEEKS. Nathaniel Weeks, also known as Nat, was born in 1791. He married Abiah Hazeltine, and they had eight children. (Courtesy of Peter Weeks, Weeks Farm Collection.)

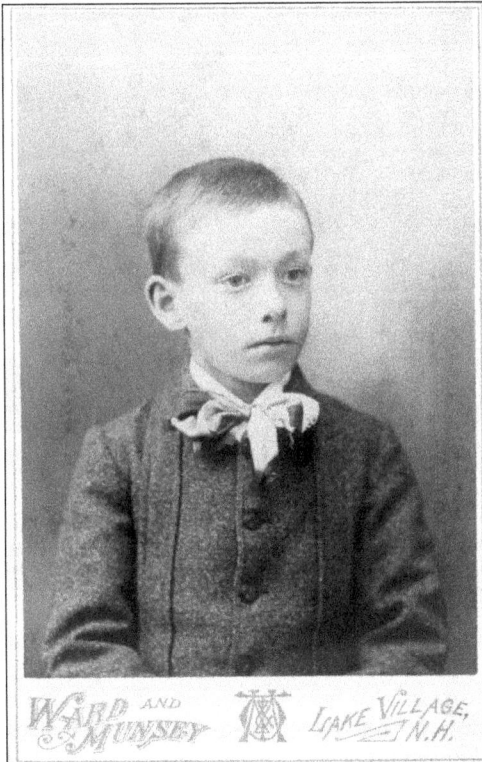

NATHANIEL WEEKS. Weeks was a member of the 10th Regiment. The men of Gilford who held regimental and higher official rank were Peasley Hoit, Ebenezer Stevens, Benjamin F. Weeks, and George W. Weeks (colonels); John M. Potter, J.Q. Merrill, and Daniel K. Smith (majors); Nathan Weeks (regimental staff officer); J.J. Morrill (general); Major Robie (drum major); and J.M. Potter (adjutant). (Courtesy of Peter Weeks, Weeks Farm Collection.)

VOTING. November 2, 1920, marked the day these women voted in Gilford. Standing just outside town hall on Potter Hill are, from left to right, Clarence Henderson, Mrs. C. Henderson, Mrs. Frank Bates, a Mrs. Goss, and Mrs. Cyrus Varney. (Courtesy of Frank Bates and Merrill Fay, Fay's Boatyard.)

ARTHUR AND MILLIE WEEKS. The Weeks Family Farm goes back many generations, and over those generations, each has done whatever they had to so that the farm would remain solvent and in the family. The tow rope that once brought in extra income was long gone by the time of this photograph. Arthur and Millie sold milk, eggs, and many other farm products. They had one son, Peter Arthur Weeks. Peter still runs the farm today. He sells hay, fresh eggs, and vegetables in season. (Courtesy of Peter Weeks, Weeks Farm Collection.)

THE SELECTMEN, 1893. Pictured here are Guilford selectmen Thomas E. Hunt, D.L. Davis, L.E. Hayward, and the treasurer, Charles F. Brown. Police service that year came to $543.73. The town clerk, Leroy M. Gould, reported 222 male dogs and 19 female dogs. The free library had $629. (Courtesy of Susan Leach.)

BERRY HUNTING, 1905. From left to right are Flo Burwell and Louise Bates Baker with Celilinda "Birdie" Bates, acting as the girls' chaperone. (Courtesy of the Thompson-Ames Historical Society.)

TINTYPE. This is an old Gilford tintype found in Mildred Weeks's hope chest, tucked and stored in the upper-right bedroom. Peter Weeks once had that bedroom as his own when he was a little boy. He believes this is his great-grandfather. (Courtesy of Peter Weeks, Weeks Farm Collection.)

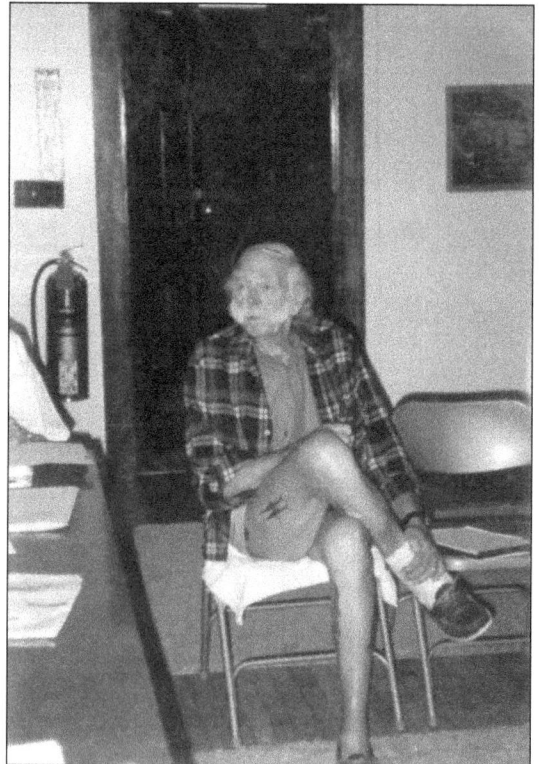

ARTHUR A. TILTON, 1917–2003. Arthur was a boat builder and carpenter. He worked for Fay's Boatyard at Smith Cove. On his farm on Old Lakes Shore Road he raised Scottish Highlanders. (Courtesy of Susan Leach.)

ARTHUR TILTON WITH NAN FAY. Arthur retired from Fay's Boatyard in 1995. He was president of the Thompson-Ames Historical Society for over seven years. He also worked with Warren Huse, author of Arcadia Publishing's *Laconia* and *Lakeport* volumes. (Courtesy of Susan Leach.)

FAMILY. Arthur Weeks and his mother are pictured here just outside the farmhouse on Weeks Road. (Courtesy of Peter Weeks, Weeks Farm Collection.)

BENJAMIN KIMBALL. Benjamin Ames Kimball was born in 1833, and when he was 15 years old, his father died. Shortly after, Benjamin joined his brother John in the Concord Machine Shop. He graduated from Dartmouth College in 1854. Benjamin then went to work for the Concord Railroad. He was the foreman and master mechanic by the time he was 26 years old. In 1870, he was elected president of the Concord Savings Bank. In 1873, he helped Concord develop a public water system. In 1876, he gave the Congregational Church a bell. Kimball represented New Hampshire in a centennial celebration in Philadelphia. He was an advisor in building the Concord Library and Historical Society Building. In 1895, he became president of the Concord & Montreal Railroad, which took over ownership of the ship *Lady of the Lakes* and retired it to Glendale to provide living quarters for the workers building the castle in 1893. When the work was completed, the ship was taken out into Glendale water and sunk. The first attempt to sink her failed, so the boat was filled with holes, and she traveled to the bottom of the bay. The ship remains a dive site today. Benjamin Kimball's son Henry died in 1919. About a year later, Benjamin died in July 1920. He is buried in the Blossom Hill Cemetery in Concord, New Hampshire. The castle was then used by his wife, Myra Tilton Elliot, and daughter-in-law Charlotte Atkinson Kimball. Once quoted as being "one of the most interesting nineteenth century homes with an imaginative use of a romantic site, a rare unaltered example of an unusual architectural style" by Don Miller, the castle has sadly begun to crumble from lack of maintenance. Today, it is listed on the "Seven to Save" in the State of New Hampshire. What was once a grand focal point of Gilford is now just a shadow of what it once was, in desperate need of tender loving care. (Courtesy of the Thompson-Ames Historical Society.)

CLASS REUNION, 1941. Beatrice Rogers (first low, far left) and Mildred Weeks (second row, far left) stand with classmates at the Belknap Recreational Area for their class reunion. (Courtesy of Peter Weeks, Weeks Farm Collection.)

GILFORD FINEST. This old photograph depicts a uniform once worn, although it is not clear who would have worn it. (Courtesy of the Thompson-Ames Historical Society.)

THE HARRIS FAMILY. From left to right, Dawn, Susan (mother), Marcia, Arthur Jr. (father), and Ty Harris are pictured here. The family's land is now the Beans and Greens Farm. (Courtesy of Susan Leach.)

DEA. HEMAN HUNTER. Born in Bristol, Maine, in 1816, Hunter came to Gilford in the winter of 1852. He ran a shingle mill on Gunstock Brook. He was a deacon of the Free Will Baptist Church and town clerk. His daughter was the first librarian in Gilford. Hunter was quoted as saying, "Our very lives dependent on steady hands, level heads, quick judgements." He was known as a kind man and lived at 30 Belknap Mountain Road. Hunter died in Gilford in 1906. (Courtesy of the Thompson-Ames Historical Society.)

ANN WEBB LEEDS. This is Esther Peter's great-grandmother. Ann's child was Ruth Dalton Leeds. Ruth (the baby) was Esther's grandmother. Ruth was born in 1891. (Courtesy of Susan Leach.)

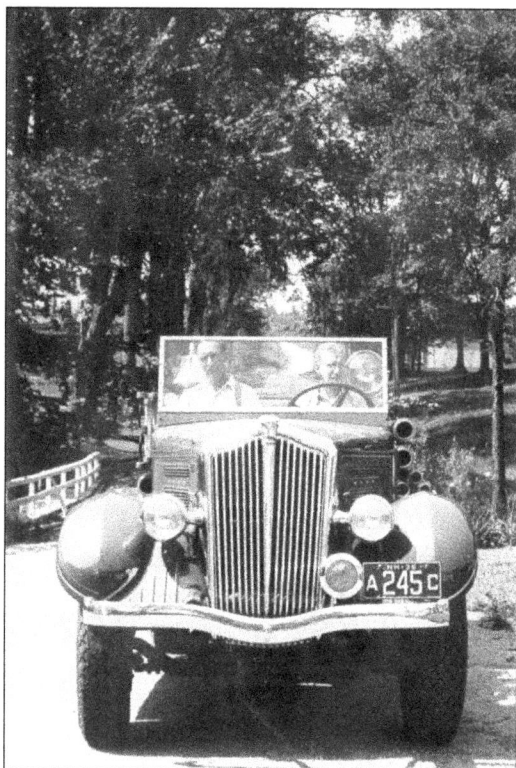

FIRST FIRE TRUCK IN GILFORD. Here is a photograph of the first fire truck to come to Gilford. The truck had 2,000 feet of hose and a portable pump. (Courtesy of Gilford Fire Rescue.)

COLBY SAWYER. Members of the Colby Sawyer family, pictured here on July 26, 1894, are, from left to right, (first row) Harry Dame, Mabel (Cady) Colby, John Dame Colby, Helen Dame, Albert Merrill, and Willis Gove; (second row) Gransier Coldy, Daniel Colby, Grammie Dame, Suzie Dame, Mary (Dame) Sawyer, and Ellen (Dame) Morrill; (third row) Carrie (Dame) Colby, Ernest Sawyer, and Susie Dame. (Courtesy of Susan Leach.)

THREE LaBONTES. Pictured are, from left to right, May, Pat, and Pete LaBonte at the Village Field during a Gilford Old Home Day. The farmers of Gilford rarely took time out from the chores and tasks that needed to be done each day. Gilford Old Home Day was a treat for the entire family because it meant a day in town or a holiday, a break from the regular routine. They would rise early to get the animals fed and cleaned. The farm equipment was silent, and each looked forward to a day of meeting with family and friends. The fun took place all day, but they had to return to the farm in the early evening to feed and care for the herds before nightfall. (Courtesy of the LaBonte Family Farm Collection, Dottie LaBonte.)

TOWN CRIERS. Gilford has had three town criers. Otto Page preceded Geoffrey Ruggles, who became the Gilford town crier for the 2012 bicentennial celebration, and he continues to make appearances on Gilford Old Home Day and special events in town. (Courtesy of the Gilford Public Library.)

WAYNE SNOW. Wayne and Shirley Snow moved to Gilford in 1957. Wayne served as a selectman, and he was inspector of elections, captain of the volunteer firefighters, a trustee of trust funds, and on the budget committee. He is an Army veteran from World War II, director of the Gilford Outing Club, commissioner of the Gilford Village Water District, and assistant town moderator. He helped to establish the board of fire engineers. (Courtesy of Gilford Fire Rescue, Bill and Sally Bickford.)

MUSICIANS. Music and musicians have been a strong part of Gilford's past. Long before the days of radio, sitting by the fire listening to the sounds of a violin or piano was a treat. Lodges and inns would often have a musician play in the evening for entertainment. Later, the Lakes Region Playhouse brought music to Gilford, and today the Bank of New Hampshire Meadowbrook Musical Pavilion accommodates musical entertainment. (Courtesy of the Thompson-Ames Historical Society.)

DRESSED FOR CHURCH. Pictured here are two women standing together by the Gilford Town Hall on Potter Hill Road. These two may have been coming from church, with their Sunday best on. The grass is tall and green, and the window to the town hall is wide open. (Courtesy of the Thompson-Ames Historical Society.)

TOWN CRIERS. Gilford has had three town criers over the years. Otto Page, one of the town criers, is pictured at right. The town criers have led the Gilford Old Home Day parade throughout time. (Courtesy of the Gilford Public Library.)

AMES FAMILY FARM. In 1855, Mary Ellen (Hayes) Ames was born in Alton, New Hampshire, and married James Noah Ames. James Noah Ames was the son of James Thompson Ames and Catherine Glidden. James Thompson Ames was a 1794 homesteader near Gunstock Brook. Mary Ellen and James Noah had four children, Herbert, Bertrand, Roger, and Maynard, who purchased an island one mile north east of the Lakeshore Farm in 1824. Mary Ellen is also Geoff Ruggles's great-grandmother. She died December 12, 1924. (Courtesy of Peter Ames, Ames Family Farm Collection.)

GRANDMA. Mary Ellen (Hayes) Ames resided in the Ames Farm Inn during the railroad era. Her parents were Ezekiel and Lydia Hayes. (Courtesy of Peter Ames and Geoff Ruggles, Ames Family Farm Collection.)

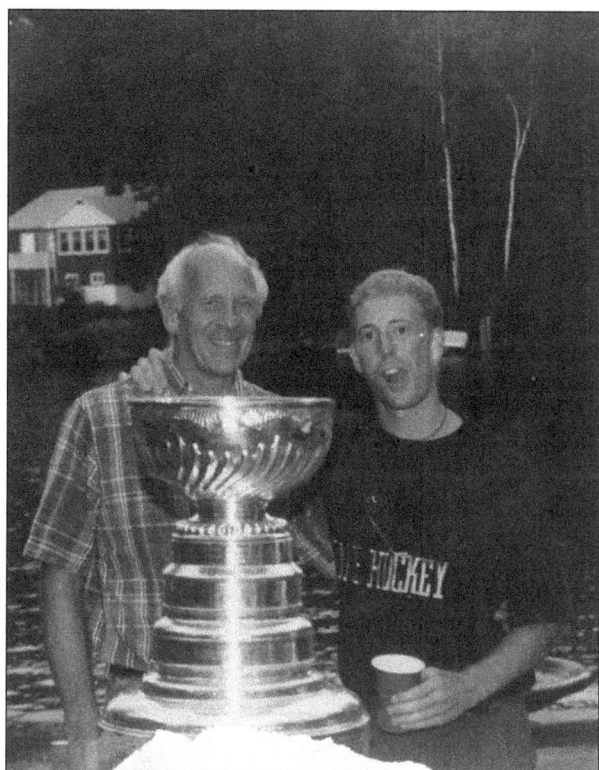

FAY'S. Pictured here with the Stanley Cup after the New Jersey Devils' win are Merrill Fay and his son William, who goes by Will. (Courtesy of Merrill Fay, Fay's Boatyard.)

MERRILL FAY, JOHN GOODHUE, ARTHUR TILTON, AND SANDY McGONAGLE, 1978. This photograph was taken at the Gilford Village Field at the Weeks Bandstand. Arthur Tilton is being given a plaque for serving so many years on the recreation commission. He later served on the zoning board of appeals. (Courtesy of the Thompson-Ames Historical Society.)

MERRILL FAY ENJOYING WINTER. This is Fay on one of his snowmobiles. Fay's Boatyard on Varney Point is a summer destination for many families returning year after year. Fay continues to work the boatyard each summer. This photograph represents one of the few times he is not working, which is a rarity. He continues to be an active force in Gilford, always protecting the history, heritage, and stories of Gilford's shorelines. His public appearances always bring a full house, as he shares his knowledge and stories of Lakes Winnipesaukee freely. (Courtesy of Merrill Fay, Fay's Boatyard.)

GILFORD FIRE RESCUE. The Gilford Fire Department is pictured here. From left to right are Alan Whitney, Sherman Thompson, Neil "Pops" Noyes, and Seely White at the dedication of the fire truck in memory of Chief Red Watson on May 23, 1968. Chief Watson had ordered the truck, a 1968 Farrar with 1,500 gallon water tank on board, for the department. (Courtesy of Gilford Fire Rescue.)

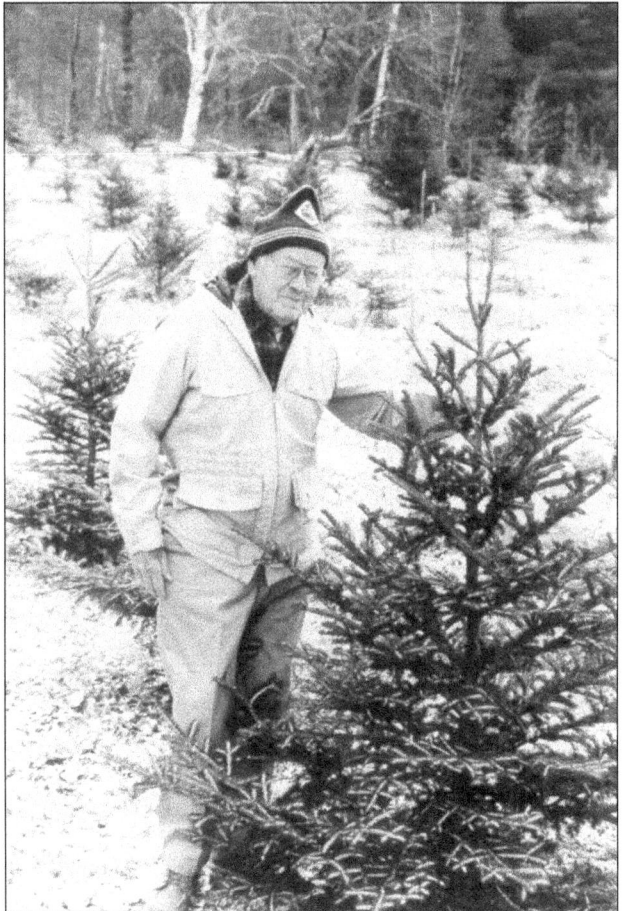

MEULKE'S TREES. Meulke Christmas Tree Farm on Belknap Mountain Road is a registered tree farm. For generations, many Gilford families have gone to the farm and tagged a Christmas tree. Shortly afterward, they return to cut the tree down and take it home to their living rooms and parlors. Pictured here is Peter Meulke. (Courtesy of the Meulke Christmas Tree Farm.)

THE SNOW FAMILY. Wayne Snow lived on Belknap Mountain Road and remained active for many years in the town. (Courtesy of Bill and Sally Bickford.)

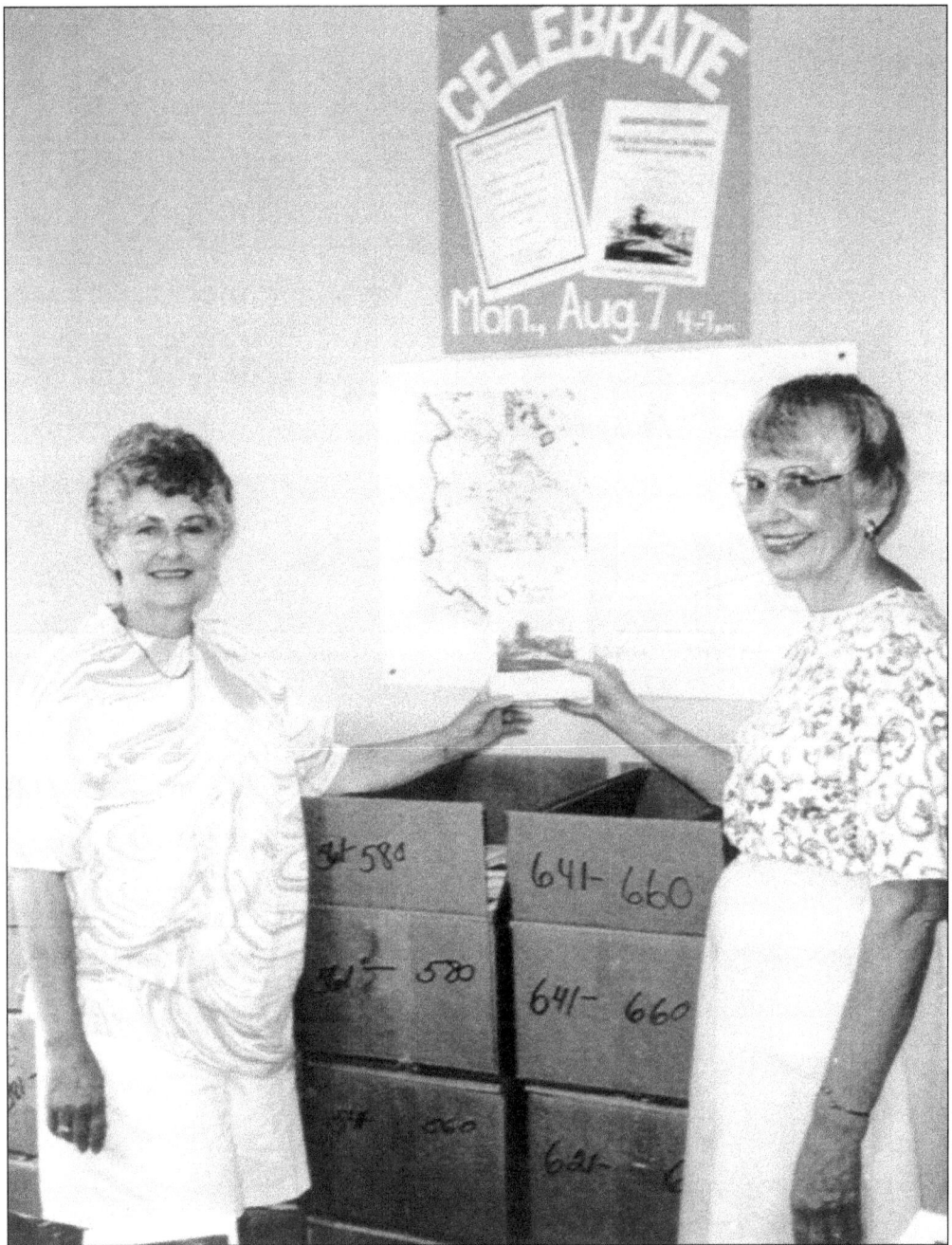

Susan Leach and Joan Nelson. Susan (left) and Joan (right) are seen here inspecting the arrival of *The Gunstock Parish*, a book by Adair Mulligan, at the Thompson-Ames Historical Society Grange building in 1995. (Courtesy of Thompson-Ames Historical Society.)

THE CUMMINGS FAMILY, 1915. Pictured here is the Cummings family. (Courtesy of Shirley Burns.)

Ten

REMEMBERING THE PAST

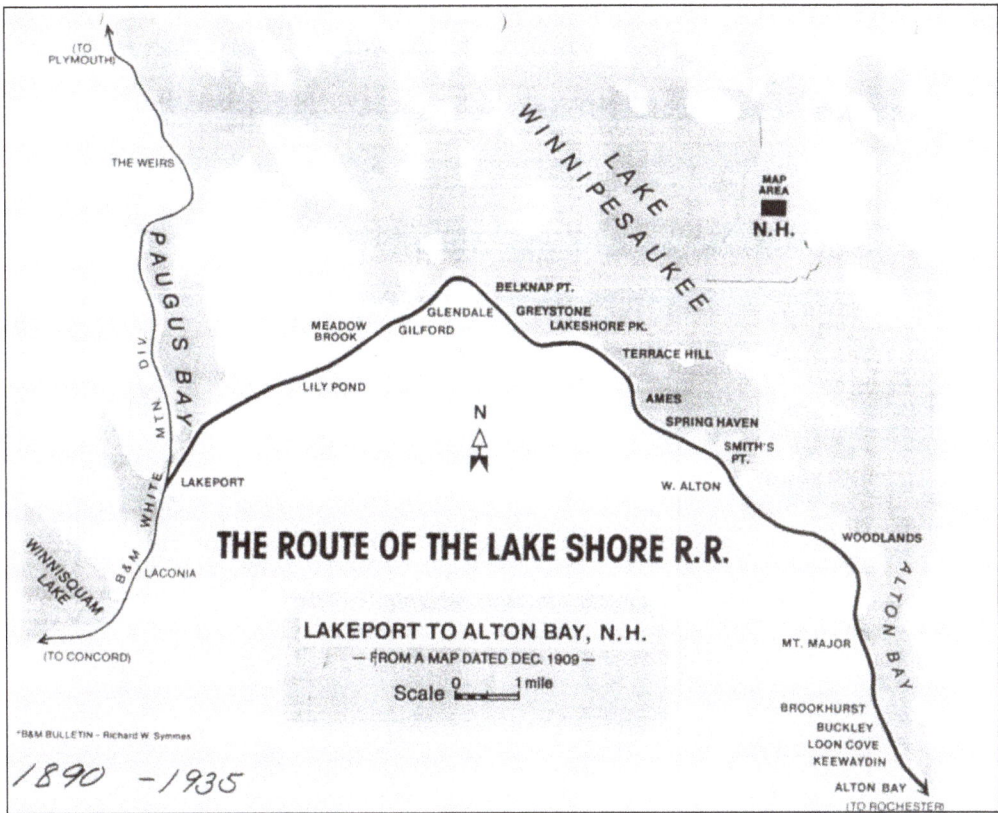

MAP OF RAILROAD. This map shows all the train stops along the Lake Shore Railroad. It also brings to light just how many of the stations on the line existed in Gilford. The railroad had a large impact on Gilford. It allowed products and goods to be transported, which improved the economy for many here. It also was the driving force behind the transition of existing strictly as an agricultural town to a vacation destination. It brought the boating in Gilford to a more commercial level. Today, Gilford is a melting pot of all its past endeavors with a strong love for the farms, plenty of rooms and places to lodge, skiing, shopping, and the beautiful lakeshores and hiking trails, with lots of places to get a great meal. (Courtesy of Susan Leach.)

THE LABONTE FAMILY. The LaBonte family owned and managed the Mountain View Farm on Hoyt Road. Pictured here are, from left to right, Robert "Bobby," Philip "Pat," Leo "Pete," Arthur, Diane, Pauline, Helen, and May. The farmhouse is very similar to the Rowe House on Belknap Mountain Road. It is a 1780 cape, with gunstock corners, and has an old stone foundation. It once had an icehouse, milking barn, and pole barn. It was originally 100 acres. The family delivered milk until 1985. (Courtesy of the LaBonte Farm Family Collection, Dottie LaBonte.)

CLARENCE DAME, POLICE OFFICER. Clarence joined the police force at an age when most men are thinking of retirement. When asked what the secret to a long life was, Dame replied, "Fresh air and outdoors, that's it." In 1941, Dame was involved in practice air-raid alerts. It was shortly after this he discovered Gilford had no record of his birth, even though he and his wife had been living in the same house he was born in. He went to the selectmen and said, "I reckon this town owes me some money." The clerk asked him why. "It seems I was never born, and a dead man can't pay taxes." Dame got his birth certificate. After World War II, he was taken off the auxiliary rolls and made a special policeman. Gilford at that time had one full-time police officer. He was also a member of the Belknap County Peace Association. He was known as a master traffic cop. "The first rule about directing traffic is to not get yourself killed!" Dame said. He also worked for the Belknap Recreational Area directing traffic and was a guard at the Sandwich Fair. At 83 years old, Clarence is the oldest police officer in the state. (Courtesy of the Gilford Police Department.)

Bolduc Church. Bolduc's Immaculate Conception Catholic Church is a traditional Catholic church. It sits across from the Bolduc Farm on Morrill Street. (Courtesy of the Bolduc Farm.)

GILFORD PUBLIC WORKS HIGHWAY GARAGE. This 1930s gambrel-roofed shed belonged to the highway department. Back then, the roads were cleared by snow rollers, which would compact the snow. (Courtesy of Sheldon C. Morgan.)

CHANGES. This building first opened up as a bank, and it sits in front of the Laconia Airport. Today, the building is known as Kitchen Cravings and is owned by the Bickford (Snow) family. The Bickfords are active members in the town, serving on various committees in Gilford and are members of the Thompson-Ames Historical Society. (Courtesy of Susan Leach.)

BELKNAP RECREATIONAL AREA. It was 1939 when the pastures belonging to the Peter, Phelp, and Sawyer families were chosen as the new recreational area site. Businessmen Oliver Colby, Charlie Carroll, and Ed Lydiard, with Congressman Fletcher Hale, all worked towards obtaining funding from the Works Progress Administration. Belknap County also helped finance the project. Originally, the area had three ski jumps, a slalom course, a toboggan chute, a warm lodge with a fireplace, and ski trails. In the summer, visitors could stay at the campground, hiking and swimming. Today, the area has evolved into the Gunstock Recreational Area. With 55 skiing trails, added lifts, events, and year-round fun, the area continues to draw visitors to Gilford every day for family fun. (Courtesy of Gunstock Recreational Area.)

THE GILFORD VILLAGE BRIDGE. At the beginning of Main Street, now Belknap Mountain Road, the Gunstock Brook (also known as Gunstock River) runs beneath the bridge. The library can be seen through the trees. On the other side of the bridge was the sight of one of Gilford's first mills. Today, one can still see the enormous stone foundation that once held the mill that brought many settlers to the area. (Courtesy of Susan Leach.)

GILFORD TANNERY HILL COVERED BRIDGE. Dedicated in 1995, the Gilford Rotary presented the bridge to the town. The Ox-K Farm brought a team of oxen to actually pull the bridge into place during the opening ceremony. Many weddings and special events have been held at the bridge. Artists and photographers stop here regularly to capture its beauty. The State of New Hampshire numbers all covered bridges, and this one was assigned No. 68. (Courtesy of Gilford Public Library.)

126

COUPLE WITH CARRIAGE. The settlers of Gilford certainly had their share of hard times, along with successes. Many generations have chosen to remain in the town, while others return each year on Gilford Old Home Day to reminisce. Gilford is a tight-knit community with historians who cherish the past, people who volunteer, and help where help is needed. (Courtesy of the Thompson-Ames Historical Society.)

Visit us at
arcadiapublishing.com

....

www.ingramcontent.com/pod-product-compliance
Lightning Source LLC
Chambersburg PA
CBHW050625110426
42813CB00007B/1723